# Prolific Thinkers' Guide

# Prolific Thinkers' Guide

Gary A. Carnow
Constance Gibson

**DALE SEYMOUR PUBLICATIONS**

*Editing: Nancy C. Tune*
*Illustrations: Rachel Gage*
*Cover Design: Lucy McCargar*

*Permission to reprint the checklist on page 23 from* SCAMPER *by Bob Eberle is kindly granted by DOK Publishers, Box 605, East Aurora, New York 14052.*

*For information about Prolific Thinking workshops, write to the authors at PROLIFIC THINKERS, 5453 E. Beverly Blvd., Los Angeles, CA 90022.*

*Originally published as* Prolific Thinkers' Guide to Prolific Thinking, *© 1984, 1986 by Prolific Thinkers.*

Order number DS13702
ISBN 0-86651-348-5

DALE
SEYMOUR
PUBLICATIONS
P.O. BOX 10888
PALO ALTO, CA 94303

6 7 8 9 10 11 12 13-MA-95 94

# Contents

*Introduction: Living on the Edge* ------------------------------ 1

*The Prolific Thinkers' Teaching Model* ------------------------ 3

*Phase One: Brainstorming, The Core of Prolific Thinking* ---- 5
SAMPLE LESSONS:
*Hatching an Idea, 9*
*Classroom Creativity Kits, 11*
*The Multipurpose Belt, 12*
*Getting the Hang of It, 14*

*Phase Two: Mind Expanders* --------------------------------- 21
SAMPLE LESSONS:
*The Ultimate Tub, 27*
*The Name of the Game, 29*

*Phase Three: Connectors* ----------------------------------- 31
SAMPLE LESSONS:
*A Sticky Business, 32*
*There's No Business Like Shoe Business, 34*
*The Thing, 36*
*The Alphabet Conspiracy, 38*

*Phase Four: Relationship Analysis* --------------------------- 39
SAMPLE LESSONS:
*The Goldberg Variations, 42*
*How to Wash a Rabbit, 45*
*Combing Through the Clues, 50*

*Prolific Thinking and Problem Solving* ----------------------- 52
SAMPLE LESSON:
*Getting in Touch with Genius, 53*

*The Prolific Thinkers' Marathon* ----------------------------- 59

*Some Final Thoughts on Prolific Thinking* -------------------- 74

*Appendix: Prolific Thinkers' Marathon Forms* --------------- 77

*Selected References* ----------------------------------------- 90

# Introduction:
# Living on the Edge

When the early pioneers crossed this country in Conestoga wagons, they couldn't stop at a filling station to repair a broken axle or reline their brakes. The settlers' survival depended on their immediate response to problem situations that few of us face today.

Perhaps early colonists in space will encounter such crises, but the fact is, we no longer live on the edge. For most of us, risk taking is not a factor in our day-to-day lives. With the diminishment of risk taking, we seem to see a decrease in creative and critical thinking, or good old-fashioned Yankee ingenuity, as well.

If we are to remain a nation of innovators, we must challenge our students with problems that will force them to think critically and to think creatively. It is our contention that these two kinds of thinking are inseparable and that they can be taught successfully.

Many of the children in our classrooms have been programmed to believe they must find the one right answer to each question. Yet we know from our own experience that most problem situations present a multiplicity of possible answers. We believe that to be effective, education must teach the process of analyzing problems, generating multiple possible solutions, and making decisions to put solutions in effect. The critical and creative thinking skills that are needed to do this must be taught separately, as well as in conjunction with particular subjects. If we do not teach these skills, we neglect an important part of the curriculum. Critical and creative thinking skills are basic to all other skills taught in school.

## Why "Prolific"?

The dictionary defines *prolific* as (1) producing young or fruit, reproductive; and (2) highly inventive, abundantly productive. We chose that term for the thinking strategies presented in this guide because it describes the ideal outcome of teaching these strategies: students who can generate multiple, highly inventive solutions to problem situations, or in effect, "prolific thinkers."

1

In order for students to think prolifically, they must learn to use a proven set of thinking strategies. Students must be taught what these strategies are and then be trained to apply them. Working from a foundation of brainstorming, students can learn specific methods for increasing their productivity and creativity through the use of patterning, classification skills, and sequential and logical thought. By practicing specific skills, students will gain the proficiency they need to apply these methods in all areas of the curriculum.

## How to Use This Guide

This guide gives you a practical framework for a hands-on approach to teaching active critical and creative thinking. Although we refer to "your students" and "your classroom" throughout, our audience is not limited to classroom teachers. Your "classroom" might be a club or troop meeting place, a day-care setting, or your own home. We especially encourage parents to use these methods with their children.

When you apply our framework, we believe the following results will occur:

- You will be able to teach creative and critical thinking skills.

- Creative and critical thinking skills and processes will make your classroom more dynamic.

- You will become a facilitator rather than a lecturer.

- Students will learn to use divergent thinking for problem solving, becoming more effective, independent learners.

This guide contains a number of resources to help you teach critical and creative thinking.

1. Use the Prolific Thinkers' Teaching Model described in these pages as a basis for developing brainstorming techniques, from spinning ideas to solving complicated problems.

2. Use the sample lessons provided in this guide as introductions to major phases in the teaching framework.

3. Use the Prolific Thinkers' Marathon described on pages 59-73 to demonstrate the application of creative and critical thinking skills in an event that's fun for everyone.

4. Use this guide as a place to record your own ideas for new or modified lessons that you find successful in your classroom.

# The Prolific Thinkers' Teaching Model

The Prolific Thinkers' Teaching Model is our guide to teaching critical and creative thinking skills. Brainstorming is the core, as well as the starting point, of the model. The core grows in size as students develop experience and skill in facing and solving problems.

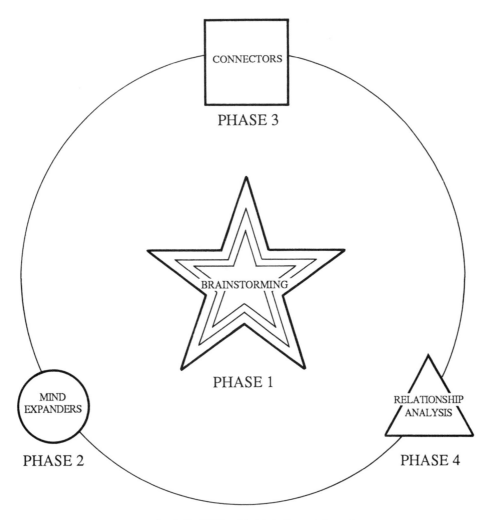

PROLIFIC THINKERS' TEACHING MODEL

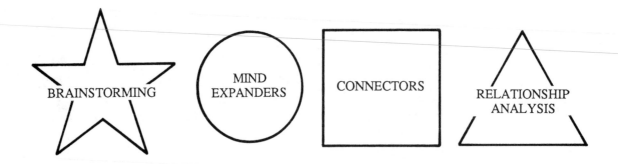

The teaching model is divided into four sections, or phases: Brainstorming, Mind Expanders, Connectors, and Relationship Analysis. These divisions are made for the purpose of teaching skills to students; we want to present one set of techniques at a time. It is especially important to begin with brainstorming because all the other techniques build on it. As you work through the phases, however, keep in mind that the process of thinking creatively and critically does not flow in a linear fashion. The phases are not meant to be used in a fixed order, and they are not exclusive of each other. You may find your students using techniques from any of the phases at any given time.

The goal of the model is to teach students a variety of thinking skills that they can choose from, combine, and modify to fit their needs whenever they face a new or unusual problem. Therefore, after working through the practice problems in the model, you should work to integrate with the rest of your curriculum the problem-solving skills taught here. In structuring your classroom lessons, consider which skills and techniques from the model are appropriate to the material you are covering.

Encourage your students to identify the elements of the model that apply to their own problem-solving situations. Once students begin to see patterns in their problem solving, all new or previously difficult learning situations become easier. The student who loves math but hates language arts may develop a more tolerant attitude once he or she discovers how to approach the subject.

Try to give students plenty of practice with their newly attained skills. The more opportunities they have to participate in brainstorming sessions, the more proficient they will become.

# *Phase One: Brainstorming, The Core of Prolific Thinking*

In order for your students to have lots of ideas, you must teach them brainstorming techniques. Brainstorming is a proven method of generating multiple ideas quickly. It activates the creative juices and generates enthusiasm for any topic.

Brainstorming sessions in your classroom will help your students become comfortable with a new kind of thinking. These sessions

- provide a setting in which students can appreciate the impact of a multiplicity of ideas rather than looking for the one "right" idea to answer a question;

- teach students to find alternative ways of solving problems;

- allow everyone in the classroom to gain facility in generating and modifying ideas; and

- teach students to listen to and appreciate each other's ideas.

We recommend that you use brainstorming daily as a warm-up activity before you teach any subject in depth. Brainstorming is also useful for reviewing material taught previously or for generating questions about the subject at hand.

# Rules for Brainstorming

These rules must be taught to the students prior to any brainstorming activity. It is a good idea to post the rules where students can see them during brainstorming sessions.

> 1. Defer all judgment.
> 2. List all ideas.
> 3. Encourage freewheeling (even if it results in outlandish ideas).
> 4. Learn to spark or piggyback on ideas.
> 5. Aim for quantity, not quality.

Before you begin your brainstorming activities, examine each rule separately with the students.

1. **Defer all judgment.** Most students are not aware of how inhibiting their remarks about each other's ideas can be or how these remarks can stifle the creative process. Be sure to discuss with the class how it feels to have one's idea labeled as "impractical" or "dumb." Try to establish a class atmosphere in which students feel free to speak up and are encouraging toward each other.

2. **List all ideas.** *All ideas* should be accepted and listed on the board to confirm their validity. Class secretaries can be selected to record the responses. Don't worry about spelling at this time. Encourage students to record the ideas in abbreviated form—just enough to get the gist of each idea. Save the elaboration for later. You may wish to have at least two secretaries to keep up with the flow of ideas. Have the secretaries take turns, recording ideas alternately, so they will not be overwhelmed by the pace. This relieves some of the anxiety that brainstorming students often experience, wondering "Will *my* idea be recorded?" In the primary grades you may wish to use an overhead projector to record ideas. This allows you to face the class but still lets the students see all their ideas in writing. Not only do kindergartners and first graders enjoy this, they are building reading skills at the same time!

3. **Encourage freewheeling.** It is important to encourage "free-wheeling," or calling out absolutely anything that comes to mind. If students are monitoring and prejudging their thoughts, the ideas won't be as abundant or as creative as they could be. Point out that many seemingly outlandish ideas have proved quite practical at a later time. Consider Jules Verne, who wrote science fiction about a journey to the moon, submarine travel, and a trip to the center of the Earth. Although his stories were strange and fantastic when he wrote them, today many of his ideas seem quite ordinary. For a closer-to-home example, remember that when the first hand-held calculators came out, most of us felt we could never afford one. Today a solar-powered calculator retails for less than five dollars!

4. **Learn to spark or piggyback on ideas.** Sparking or piggybacking occurs when a student thinks of an alternative to or modification of another student's idea. For example, in the sample warm-up lesson that follows, students think of uses for a Leggs "egg" hosiery container. One student might suggest using it as a candy dish. Other students, thinking in terms of a receptacle, might suggest the egg be used to hold a plant or cotton balls. Expanding on the idea, someone else might suggest it be used as an egg separator or a measuring cup. As students have encounters with piggybacking during brainstorming sessions, they will develop more flexibility in their thinking.

5. **Aim for quantity, not quality.** By stressing the need for quantity over quality in brainstorming, you encourage students to take some risks and participate. Daring to have an idea recorded is essential to the brainstorming process. This is precisely the message you must send out to the class. Encourage students to keep their ideas coming, including apparently impractical or fantasy-based ideas. This helps to create the freewheeling atmosphere needed for effective critical and creative thinking in the classroom. When students can contribute their ideas freely and comfortably, they are well on their way to developing expertise in brainstorming.

## *Listening and Questioning During Brainstorming*

Students must develop good listening habits during brainstorming sessions. Repeating an idea that has already been suggested serves no useful purpose and can stop the flow of ideas. The student who is presenting an idea must speak clearly, and other students must listen to each contribution. Careful listening is also important for sparking or piggybacking and for establishing a cooperative atmosphere within the class.

Also essential to good brainstorming is the teacher's ability to ask provocative, open-ended questions. Good questions will motivate students to think critically and creatively. By asking for alternatives, new endings, or a prediction, a teacher can keep the students' imaginations involved.

## Notes on Brainstorming with Concrete Objects

In order to accustom students to the rules for brainstorming and to increase the quantity of their responses, you may want to start your brainstorming sessions with a warm-up exercise. These exercises are especially effective when you use a concrete object such as the plastic egg in the activity that follows.

When students are brainstorming about a concrete object, have them demonstrate the uses they suggest for the object. Encourage them to move the object around and look at it from many perspectives. This will help students escape an obvious pitfall—fixed functionalism, or the assumption that the way something is *typically* used is also the *only* way it can be used. For example, in the lesson "Hatching an Idea," students may see the egg-shaped container only as a receptacle for objects. However, the egg could just as easily become a nose cone for a rocket, a pattern for drawing a circle, a cookie cutter, a miniature igloo, a sand castle mold, or perhaps a protective cover for a broken toe.

# *Hatching an Idea*

**BRAINSTORMING**

*Tools of the Trade*
Half of a Leggs "egg" hosiery container

*Time*
10 minutes

*Problem*
Give as many uses of the plastic egg as you can.

*Procedure*

1. Review the rules for brainstorming.

2. Begin the session by making a suggestion (for example, "It could be used as an elbow guard") and passing the container to the first student. Each student makes a suggestion and passes the container on.

3. Encourage students to demonstrate how the item is used in each idea. For example, if you suggest an elbow guard, place the container over your elbow.

*Teacher Tips*

Start your own collection of concrete objects for warm-up brainstorming sessions. Half a tennis ball, a light bulb, walnut shells, or Tupperware gadgets make great "unknowns." As homework, challenge students to find and bring in an "unknown" or a mystery object that could be used for class brainstorming.

## Notes on Applying Ideas

Once your students have learned the rules of brainstorming and are gaining experience in generating ideas, they are ready to expand their skill by applying their ideas. The following lessons are suggested for such practice.

The lesson "Classroom Creativity Kits" helps students see their ideas applied in a concrete manner in the classroom. This lesson involves little or no cost. It offers students who are clever with their hands an opportunity to show ingenuity that may not be apparent in their oral or written classroom work.

"The Multipurpose Belt" is a lesson to develop creativity. Students use materials they find and brainstorm ideas to develop unique products.

# *Classroom Creativity Kits*

BRAINSTORMING

## *Tools of the Trade*

A collection of found objects: tops of aerosol cans, empty plastic containers, rubber bands, paper clips, labels, string or yarn, index cards, nuts and bolts, plastic or Styrofoam cups, flexible wire, tinker toys, Popsicle sticks, plastic containers, and so on

## *Time*

At least 45 minutes

## *Problem*

Use the found objects to make (1) something useful, (2) a musical instrument, or (3) a new toy. The problem can be changed weekly, using these suggestions and others of your own devising.

## *Procedure*

1. Review the rules for brainstorming with your students.

2. You may have students work in pairs or triads so they can bounce their ideas off each other. This gives the less successful students an opportunity to observe risk taking and the trial-and-error process in a safe setting.

# *The Multipurpose Belt*

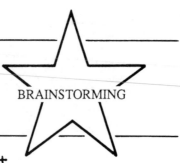

BRAINSTORMING

Interplanetary Explorer's Belt

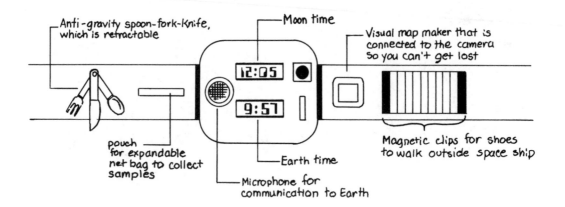

*Tools of the Trade*
Materials will vary depending on the kinds of belts
the students design.

*Time*
One class brainstorming session, followed by two
or three sessions for design and model creation

*Problem*
Design a multipurpose belt that is useful for
workers in a particular occupation.

*Procedure*
Present this scenario to the students:

> *We are employed in a new factory that makes multipurpose belts
> for workers who do a variety of jobs. You are a designer.
> Design a belt for a specific job; then make a model of the belt
> with all its special features. You will want to make a drawing
> first to help you determine what equipment and materials you
> will need to complete your model. In your drawing, be sure to
> label all the parts and explain their uses.*

## *Notes on Role Playing*

In the lesson "The Multipurpose Belt," we use role playing to help orient the students to the assignment. Role playing helps them be less inhibited in their thinking. It offers a protective covering for risk taking, because the student is functioning not as him- or herself but as a character with a specific purpose.

Whenever you present a scenario for role playing, remember that your enthusiasm will help the students remove themselves from the classroom and get into the fantasy situation you are creating. With younger students, we often put a magical inflection in our voices: "Boys and girls, in a moment I'm going to turn around, and when I face you again I will no longer be your teacher. Instead, I will be your boss, Philo T. Bell, the owner of the Prolific Thinkers' Telephone Company." When you have finished saying this, your students' faces will tell you that they know this is going to be a very special lesson.

In the next brainstorming lesson, "Getting the Hang of It," role playing is used to involve the students in a cooperative venture. Students assume roles of workers with divergent points of view.

# *Getting the Hang of It*

BRAINSTORMING

*Tools of the Trade*
Butcher paper, marking pens

*Time*
10 minutes for primary grades
20 minutes for upper grades

*Problem*
How could you improve the dial telephone?
(Various problems could be posed for this
kind of activity; the only requirements are
that the problem be open-ended and have
many solutions.)

*Procedure*
Present this scenario to the students. You play the part of a factory owner
addressing a meeting of the factory's designers, advertising personnel, and
executives.

> *I've brought all of you together today because the public is not
> buying our dial telephones. Women complain that they break
> their fingernails when dialing. The pushbutton phones are much
> faster. I could give a dozen reasons why our dial phones aren't
> selling, but the point is, we are facing bankruptcy. I've gathered
> you here for one purpose. Our jobs are on the line. We have to
> find a new way to improve our product or recycle its parts—or
> we will be forced to close the factory.*

*Teacher Tips*
Help students get started by discussing the different points of view the
role playing will have them take. For example, ask, "Will the designer and
the person in charge of advertising approach this problem in the same way?
How will their approaches differ? How will the salespeople approach the
problem?"

Many activities can be used as follow-up for this lesson. Blueprints and
drawings of new products can be developed with the parts labeled. The
products can be named. A price to the public can be determined and an

advertising campaign developed. Because the lesson involves the telephone company, your class might even want to write letters to the local phone company offering their suggestions. The extensions and possibilities are limited only by your imagination. Bounce your ideas around with a colleague or let your students develop their own original follow-ups.

---

## Scenarios for Further Brainstorming

"The Multipurpose Belt" and "Getting the Hang of It" can be adapted to fit your own personality. The scenarios for both lessons can be altered to allow the actor in you to come out. You know your classroom better than anyone else. The scenarios and lessons that really spark your students will vary from group to group, and even from week to week. So many variables are operative in a classroom. However, we find that when our own enthusiasm is high, it generates an energy that is contagious, and success is guaranteed.

The brainstorming scenarios you explore in your classroom should tap your own expertise and imagination. We try to choose scenarios that
- are open-ended in nature,
- allow for multiple responses, and
- can be transferred to a concrete kinesthetic project.

Both "The Multipurpose Belt" and "Getting the Hang of It" give your students the opportunity to work individually or in small groups to create products that reflect their creative thinking.

Our ideas for scenarios are triggered by brainstorming. Some are sparked by something we have read, a hobby or interest, or a new area of study. Students like to create their own scenarios for brainstorming. The following scenarios have been tested in our own classrooms and have met with great success.

### The No-Drip Ice-Cream Cone

Chocolate-chocolate chip, look out! Through hard work and Yankee ingenuity, you have discovered the ultimate food product, ice cream that doesn't need to be kept in the freezer! This ice cream stays cold and solid. It won't melt, even on the hottest day. Your job now is to develop an ad campaign to introduce this "chilling" discovery to an ice-cream loving public. You must plan all strategies for the campaign, including naming the product, developing novel ways to let the world know what it has been missing, and planning the packaging of the product. Dessert may never be the same.

### A Surprising Decree!

The Board of Education has issued a very surprising decree. You have been selected to be the principal for 24 hours, starting Monday. During your time as principal you may put rules in force, change procedures, plan programs, and make any necessary alterations to your school to fulfill your expectations. As the principal, it is your duty to improve the curriculum; you have the power to do whatever it takes to accomplish that. Remember, 24 hours pass quickly. What are your actions?

### Move Over, Henry Ford

Henry Rabbit Ford, president of Road Rabbit Limited, creator of the Model R car, has developed a new automobile for today's demanding driver. The production line is ready to roll, but first, as members of the design team, we must suggest a list of options available on the Model R. We must keep in mind that the Model R driver represents an upwardly mobile consumer who demands the latest technology. We at Road Rabbit Limited are committed to providing tomorrow's technology today. We know that the design team will develop options that will make the Model R the most fabulous car in automotive history!

### TV Program Planner

A shake-up at NBZ-TV has radically changed your life! Handpicked from the mailroom, you are now the head of scheduling for NBZ and have the power to put on television anything you want! What new shows can we expect? This Friday you must announce your first fall lineup. The NBZ stockholders will be listening intently to your choices. After all, your experience and track record are nonexistent! If you're a hit, your rags-to-riches story could inspire the entire television industry!

## Starter Ideas for Brainstorming

In making a list of questions to brainstorm, you may hesitate to include some ideas because they seem too obvious. Other ideas may seem hackneyed to you, and still others seem too far out. Yet it is essential to include anything that comes to mind, so you will have plenty of ideas to piggyback on and spark the imagination. Use the following list as a place to write down your own ideas as you practice brainstorming. Many of the ideas can be expanded into scenarios. Mark the ones that interest you and jot down your ideas for scenarios. Soon you will have your own personal resource for every day of the year.

---

How would you . . .

weigh a whale?

weigh a piano?

pull a tiger's tooth?

design the perfect room?

rewrite the rules for Monopoly?

solve the transportation problems in your city?

keep gangs off the street and out of trouble?

---

How would you improve . . .

| | |
|---|---|
| a water cooler? | a toy robot? |
| a typewriter? | a pencil? |
| a schoolyard? | the bathtub? |
| fast food service? | shoes? |

---

What if . . .

we had two heads?

no one could read?

there were no electricity?

we all looked alike?

we lived our lives backward?

we had no nose?

all children stopped growing at three feet?

we didn't need any sleep?

our stuffed animals could talk?

---

Name as many things as you can that are. . .
   green and edible.
   soft and white.
   hard and can float.
   sticky and can change shape.
   nice to look at and easy to break.

Name as many things as you can that . . .
   float.
   attract.
   come in pairs.
   include the word *ship.*
   bounce and won't break.
   contain a color word, such as "red tape."
   are red, white, and blue.
   have repeated patterns in nature.

Give as many uses as you can for . . .
   a carrot.                    dental floss.
   a toothpick.                 a chair.
   a brick.                     a tin can.
   a paper clip.                a Leggs container.
   a bottle cap.                a light bulb.
   a hairpin.                   a pill bottle.
   a pair of socks.             a plastic soft-drink container.
   a garbage bag.               a broom.
   a coat hanger.               a piece of rope.

Design a new. . .
   spoon.                       mailbox.
   chair.                       dish.
   swing.                       vitamin.
   telephone.                   breakfast food.
   backscratcher.               table.
   exercise machine.            type of clothing.
   toy.                         musical instrument.

18

How many ways can you . . .

| | |
|---|---|
| open a jar? | play a game with a ball? |
| earn money? | wrap a present? |
| use paper? | thank someone? |
| make a friend? | communicate with another person? |

Make up a story that includes . . .

a space alien, a garbage collector, a palm tree, and a watermelon.

a teacher, a sunflower seed, a swimming pool, and a ten-gallon hat.

a home computer, an inquisitive child, and magic.

Describe. . .

a new sandwich.

a home under the sea.

a new form of currency.

a sundae with unusual ingredients.

a new postal system.

a new cafeteria at your school.

Give directions for . . .

walking without gravity.

making a peanut butter sandwich.

getting to your school if someone is flying.

finding your way to the library.

Draw a map . . .

of a new type of amusement park.

of the ideal playground.

for your pet to find its way home.

of the best kid's room ever.

How could you recycle . . .

dial telephones?

garbage pails?

Popsicle sticks?

containers from McDonalds?

Coin a new word for . . .

a two-dollar bill.           a space-age dance craze.

a lazy student.           a remote-control telephone.

a television viewer.        a new soft drink.

a computer wizard.        a computer dictionary.

If I were . . .

a wild animal, I'd be a _____ because . . .

a foreign country, I'd be _____ because . . .

a machine, I'd be a _____ because . . .

a musical instrument, I'd be a _____ because . . .

a dessert, I'd be _____ because . . .

a cartoon character, I'd be _____ because . . .

# *Phase Two: Mind Expanders*

MIND
EXPANDERS

After students have experienced a few brainstorming lessons and have some facility for generating ideas, mind-expanding techniques may be introduced. In brainstorming, we follow set rules to generate ideas. With mind-expanding techniques, we bring in some new sets of rules to help keep the ideas flowing. Mind expanders are different ways of organizing our thoughts to get a fresh look at a problem and, ideally, generate fresh ideas. We like to refer to the following models during this phase:

- FFOE, an acronym for the terms *fluency, flexibility, originality,* and *elaboration.*

- SCAMPER, another acronym, borrowed from Bob Eberle and explained in detail in the following pages.

- Incubation techniques, especially useful when a lull occurs during brainstorming.

All of these can help the teacher of prolific thinking to expand and revitalize the creative thinking process.

## *Guidelines for Fostering Creativity: FFOE*

The FFOE model is based on the ideas of J. P. Guilford and E. Paul Torrance. Their books and articles have stimulated much interest among teachers who wish to increase creativity in their classrooms. We like the FFOE model, a combination of the Guilford and Torrance works, because it offers an outline of reminders to help you unlock creative thought and encourage problem solving. FFOE describes four attributes or types of responses we should be looking for when students are brainstorming, as follows:

- **Fluency**—the generation of as many ideas and responses as possible. The goal is a large number of ideas, suggestions, products, or plans. The wider the range of ideas, the greater the fluency. Fluent people have many diverse interests and abilities. They possess the raw material from which to build new ideas.

- **Flexibility**—the ability to make associations, to skip categories, and to adapt objects or ideas to new uses. Flexible people also have the ability to combine many kinds of information in many different ways.

- **Originality**—the production of unique and unusual ideas or combinations of ideas. Original people have the ability to make remote associations and to see unusual twists to problem-solving situations.

- **Elaboration**—the embellishment of ideas with details, often through the creation of systems and models.

Any teacher can use FFOE to foster creative thinking in students. Unlike the other mind-expanding techniques we present here, FFOE is not taught directly to students. Instead, teachers simply keep FFOE in mind as they guide students' brainstorming experiences. That is, during brainstorming sessions we encourage students to look at objects or ideas in new ways to increase the *fluency* and *flexibility* of their responses. A variety of possibilities emerge during brainstorming, and we remain on the lookout for *originality,* ready to grab and encourage that unique "new" idea when it surfaces. Later we encourage *elaboration,* with follow-up activities such as designing and building models. In short, FFOE serves to remind us of our creative objectives during brainstorming. It is an outline teachers can refer to time and again.

Be aware that originality, certainly the most important aspect of creativity, is also one of the most difficult to judge. To the child who has never heard of a transformer, a toy that converts from a lion to a robot may be an original idea. In the Prolific Thinkers' Marathon there is an activity called "Mental Gymnastics" in which student teams demonstrate their proficiency at brainstorming. "Mental Gymnastics" encourages fluency, flexibility, and originality. During this activity, judges rate each response as either "common" or "unique," with unique responses receiving more points. In our tournaments, we always have two judges and take a total of their ratings in order to minimize the effect of subjective judgment. Like our judges, you will likely find during classroom brainstorming that it's not always easy to ascertain what is really a unique and original response. As you teach the sample lessons, however, you will come to recognize answers that are "original" for a specific grade level, age, or individual.

## SCAMPER, *or Fifty More Ways to Improve the Telephone*

The suggestion box was invented in the 1890s to improve communication between workers and management. This innovation was probably the greatest all-time generator of the "what if" question. Eberle, in 1971, used the "what if" approach in devising SCAMPER. SCAMPER is a mnemonic device for the different ways that students can expand and revitalize their thinking during brainstorming. As they think of the words *substitute* (S) and *combine* (C), for example, they ask themselves such questions as "What if I *substituted* this . . .?" and "What would happen if I *combined* that with . . .?" Eberle's checklist is adapted from the work of Alex F. Osborn (see "Selected References," page 90).

| S C A M P E R Checklist | | |
|---|---|---|
| S | Substitute | Have a thing or person act or serve in another's place. |
| C | Combine | Bring together or unite. |
| A | Adapt | Adjust to suit a condition or purpose. |
| M | Modify | Alter or change in form or quality. |
| | Magnify | Enlarge or make greater in quality or form. |
| | Minify | Make smaller, lighter, slower, less frequent. |
| P | Put to other uses | Use for purposes other than the one intended. |
| E | Eliminate | Remove, omit, or get rid of a quality, part, or whole. |
| R | Rearrange | Change order or adjust; create another layout or scheme. |

To demonstrate SCAMPER's application, look at a list of brainstormed ideas—for example, the list of ideas generated for the telephone lesson, "Getting the Hang of It." See how your ideas change and expand when you systematically apply each verbal command.

For example, what could you *substitute* for the receiver on the dial telephone? One student suggested headphones, similar to those on his pocket radio, on a very long cord. This would allow the individual complete freedom with his or her hands during an extended conversation. Piggybacking on this idea, a young girl who didn't like the idea of having her hair messed up suggested an earplug instead. This device would be similar to a hearing aid and could be cordless.

Once you have introduced SCAMPER, keep a chart of the key words posted in the classroom where students can refer to it easily. "The Ultimate Tub" lesson on page 27 demonstrates how to apply SCAMPER to a brainstorming session.

## Techniques for Incubating Ideas

After the warm-up process in a brainstorming session, ideas usually flow so quickly that it is difficult to record them all. But after the initial responses, a lull may occur.

This lull is a natural part of the prolific thinking process. The brain has been bombarded by an overabundance of information to be sifted and sorted in a short period of time. The lull can serve as an incubation period. During

this period, the mind can categorize the ideas that have been recorded, putting them in some kind of order. The students will then be ready to compare their ideas with those previously generated. From this process new ideas will emerge.

Allow time for this incubation period. It is perfectly all right for a silent period to occur in the classroom while students review and think about the material they have generated.

Here are some techniques that you can use to continue the incubation process and generate even more new ideas.

1. **Review.** Go over the recorded responses with the class. You might have a student read them aloud. Hearing those ideas will likely help someone in the classroom gain new insight or piggyback on an idea.

2. **Try the ABC connection.** If the class is really stuck, ask students to go from *A* to *Z* looking for new responses. For example:

   *A* . . . the *alphabet* on the telephone dial could be changed to pictures.

   *B* . . . the *bell* could be changed to a flashing light or a musical theme.

   In other words, use the alphabet to identify physical characteristics or to trigger associations that might generate additional responses.

3. **Contribute.** The teacher should be a part of the brainstorming process. During incubation, contribute your own ideas. You can direct the class's approach into new channels or perspectives simply by participating in this process. For example, we always have no difficulty thinking of ways that the object or idea under discussion—whatever it may be—could be used as a diet aid. (Did you know that the Leggs container is the perfect measuring device for three-fourths of an ounce of dry cereal on the Weight Watcher's program?)

4. **Record on butcher paper.** For long-term projects, try recording your answers on butcher paper. We like colored paper with contrasting felt markers for added interest. After the brainstorming session, this paper can be moved to another area of the room. Encourage students to record any new answers on the paper throughout the day. Refer to the butcher paper the next day. Students may find that some good new ideas have been incubating overnight. Some of the world's greatest inventors solved problems in their dreams. Who knows, you may be encouraging the next Thomas Edison!

## The Pigeon-Hole Phenomenon

Devices such as SCAMPER and the incubation techniques help students by providing a format or template that can be applied systematically to increase creative thinking. With practice in brainstorming, students often discover for themselves categories that they can apply to many situations. This is an important ability because it lets students approach new problems with tools that they know will work. However, there is a pitfall in this process that we call "the pigeon-hole phenomenon."

While applying given categories to problem solving is a useful skill, it can become a rote exercise that stifles rather than enhances thinking. If students begin to approach all problems with the same formula, they will lose their spontaneity and diversity of thought and channel their thinking too narrowly.

You can reopen the flow of thought by discussing the problem and encouraging students to list the categories they are currently using. The class can discuss various ways to use those categories and ways to change the categories, adapting them to each new problem.

# The Ultimate Tub

MIND
EXPANDERS

*Tools of the Trade*
Graph paper, pencil, eraser

*Time*
One class brainstorming session and
20-minute follow-up period

*Problem*
What would you include in the design
of the ultimate bathtub?

*Follow-up*
Draw and label the parts of your
ultimate tub.

*Procedure*

1. Review the elements of SCAMPER.

2. Conduct a brainstorming session for this problem, listing responses on the
   board or on butcher paper. Leave plenty of space under each response.

3. Have students apply SCAMPER to the listed items and add their new ideas
   to the responses already recorded.

*Sample Responses*
Here is a sampling of responses you might get from the initial brainstorming
session:

- rubberized soft material
- nonelectric telephone
- built-in pillow
- ice box
- seats on sides
- sun lamps
- liquid soap dispenser

- eight feet by ten feet, and six feet deep
- nonslip bottom
- gold
- built-in TV and video cassette player
- spigot for soft drinks
- colored water
- back washer

Using SCAMPER as a systematic reminder of ways to generate new ideas or modify existing ones, your class might come up with a list similar to this one, which was generated by a group of fifth graders.

| | | |
|---|---|---|
| S | Substitute | Instead of seats on the side, have tub contoured to the body for maximum comfort. |
| C | Combine | Combine the rubberized soft material with a grooved surface on the bottom of the tub to prevent slipping and falling. Add a handrail to the side wall. |
| A | Adapt | Create an entertainment center with TV, video cassette player, and special book holder and page turner for people who prefer to read in the bathtub. A robotic hand turns the pages so they won't get wet. |
| M | Modify | Modify the sunlamp so that it is in the sides and bottom of the tub as well as overhead for an all-over tan. |
| | Magnify | Add movable partitions to the tub so it can be made larger. |
| | Minify | Move partitions to make the tub smaller, depending upon the amount of time you have for your bath. |
| P | Put to other uses | Use the enlarged tub to practice aerobic exercises and avoid muscle strain and sweating. |
| E | Eliminate | Eliminate spigots on tubs. Water enters tub from jets in the sides. |
| R | Rearrange | Locate tubs in the family room, where family members can relax together while they watch TV. Movable side walls will automatically enclose tub for privacy when desired. |

---

# The Name of the Game

MIND
EXPANDERS

*Tools of the Trade*
Paper, pencils

*Time*
One class brainstorming session and a block of time for follow-up
(could be done as homework)

*Problem*
Name a new product, invention, idea, or discovery. Some examples
you may wish to explore: a new chewy potato chip, a newly
discovered planet in the universe, a new automobile, a new simulation
board game that involves the stock market, or a portable lap-top
personal computer.

*Follow-up*
Prepare a campaign to sell the product. Create a print ad for a
magazine.

*Procedure*

1. Hold a discussion about the qualities of successful names. These often
   share some of the characteristics of the best-known names around the
   globe, such as Coca-Cola, Xerox, and Kodak.
   - Successful names often begin and end with the same letter.
   - They tend to use "explosive" consonants, such as K, P, Q, and V. These
     make words stand out in ordinary speech.
   - Successful names often suggest the images the product should evoke.

2. Present this scenario to the students:
   *We are the Prolific Propagators, a consulting firm that
   specializes in naming new products and inventions. Our goal is*

*to provide our clients with a name that has that special zing, the
zing needed to make a new product visible and to get consumers
excited about it. Today our task is to provide a moniker for . . .*

3. Brainstorm. Use a prototype or a picture to illustrate a product or
discovery. If you are brainstorming a name for an idea, be sure to
describe the idea fully to your students.

*Teacher Tips*

1. Keep FFOE in mind. Encourage students to be flexible in the ways they
think about the product to be named.

2. Withhold judgment and save elaboration until later.

3. Be aware that often this kind of brainstorming branches off into related
areas. For example, in trying to name a new potato chip, we may need to
consider what market we are trying to attract, the competition that exists
today, the price of the product, and the uniqueness of the product. All
these factors may affect the naming process.

4. As an extension, have your students bring in well-known product names
that follow the naming practices listed above. Try to identify some other
techniques that were used. Can you find examples of companies or
products that have picked up on a national trend or fascination? A
product that is named because of its seasonal use? Can you think of other
ways to classify the names you've found? Bring in print advertisements
for products whose names have come to be household words. Discuss
ways in which advertisements use the names visually and in the copy to
create a strong, integrated effect.

# Phase Three: Connectors

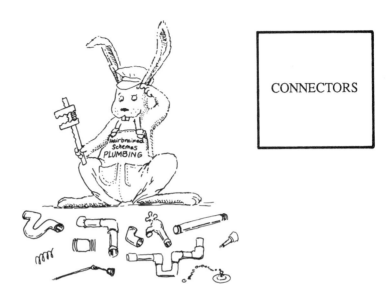

Connectors help us to see the relationships among elements of a problem. They also enable us to analyze the elements and make new connections in a creative manner. In order to make connections, students must know how to list the attributes or properties of an object and how to classify objects and ideas. Attribute listing helps students to

- break down a problem for detailed examination,
- note differences and similarities among elements of a problem, and
- begin to build new configurations, combining elements of a problem in a new way.

Classifying helps students to

- discover structure and order that is not readily apparent,
- see potential ways of producing new connections, and
- hypothesize about unknowns and make predictions.

Attribute listing is an easy way to begin classifying information at the concrete level. A good approach is to start with the five senses. This is done in the following lesson, "A Sticky Business."

# A Sticky Business

*Tools of the Trade*
Chewels gum, one piece per student. (We use Chewels because it is a gum-candy combination with more than one flavor, but the exact item is not important. Any edible item that appeals to the students will work.)

*Time*
15 minutes

*Problem*
Tell all you can about this object using your five senses.

*Procedure*

1. Review and list the five senses on the board or on butcher paper.

2. Tell students they are going to generate all the information they can about the gum. Advise them to approach the object as an unknown. That way they can concentrate on what their senses tell them, not on what they already know about the gum.

3. Begin with the sense of sight. Ask students for all the information they can generate about the appearance of the object.

4. Continue brainstorming with touch, smell, sound, and taste.

5. List all the attributes of the object until you feel the students have exhausted most of the obvious responses. You may wish to list their responses on a chart like the one shown on page 33.

# Chart for Attribute Listing

## Look

*Shape?* _____

*Color?* _____

*Size?* _____

*Thick/thin?* _____

_____

## Feel

*Texture?* _____

*Weight?* _____

*Solid/liquid?* _____

*Temperature?* _____

_____

## Sound

*Sound it makes?* _____

*Sounds made by using it?* _____

_____

## Smell

*Pleasant/unpleasant?* _____

*Acid, sweet, sour, floral?* _____

_____

## Taste

*Salty, sweet, sour, bitter?* _____

*Location on your tongue?* _____

_____

_____

## Miscellaneous

*Parts of the object?* _____

*Uses for the object?* _____

*Materials object is made of?* _____

_____

_____

## *There's No Business Like Shoe Business* | CONNECTORS

*Tools of the Trade*
No special materials are necessary.

*Time*
Approximately 20 minutes

*Problem*
How many ways can you categorize shoes?

*Procedure*

1. Have the students form a large circle with their chairs.

2. Ask the students to remove their shoes and place them in the center of the circle.

3. Present this scenario to the students:

   *We have hired Patience T. Rabbit to manage our shoe store. Unfortunately we have had some unreliable help lately, and when Ms. Rabbit arrived in the store today, she found all the shoes dumped in a pile on the floor. Patience knows that she needs to organize the shoes in some fashion, but she doesn't wear shoes herself so her ideas may not be the first ones that would come to our minds. How many ways can she organize these shoes?*

4. To start this activity, put all the blue shoes together. Have students raise their hands when they think they have discovered the secret to your organization. The student who guesses the correct method takes your place and organizes the shoes in a different way.

5. All sorts of creative categories can develop, such as type of fasteners, style of shoe, heel height, size, material the shoes are made of, texture of soles, and so on.

6. A follow-up activity might include writing shoe riddles. In what professions do people wear special shoes?

# Notes on Developing Patterning

Lessons like the two preceding ones, "A Sticky Business" and "There's No Business Like Shoe Business," give students a handle on two different aspects of Connectors:

- searching for generalizations that apply to all the objects in a group, and
- looking for general categories or attributes that are frequently used to organize objects.

In both lessons, the attributes used to describe objects are the same. Size, color, shape, and texture are standard terms with which we describe unknowns as well as known objects.

SCAMPER demonstrates how we use these terms in brainstorming. For example, *minify* and *magnify* relate to the attributes of shape, size, weight, and so on. You can demonstrate this to students by having them name as many attributes as they can of a given item. After the attributes are listed on the board, have students label each one with the sense it relates to. For this activity, look for an item that will appeal to several senses, such as a food item or a toy that makes noise.

Set up centers where students can practice classifying. Supply the centers with collections of such things as different kinds of paper fasteners, nails and screws, paint chip samples, bottle tops, buttons, fabric and wood samples, and sets of flatware.

With practice, your students will be able to think of new categories to fit not only physical items, but words and figures as well.

# *The Thing*

*Tools of the Trade*
Wax paper, plastic knife, Fruit Roll-Ups in an unusual flavor such as apricot, a record sheet

*Time*
20 to 30 minutes

*Problem*
Write a news report on a strange "Thing" that is threatening your town. Devise a plan to wipe out this Thing.

*Procedure*

1.  Present this scenario to the students:

    *You are a reporter for the local newspaper. You have been sent to investigate a report of an unknown substance that has invaded your community. The substance alternately eats everything in its path while growing at a rapid rate, then shrinks back into a small blob. When you arrive at the scene, all that remains of the Thing is what you see on your desk. You must record all the factual information about the Thing that you possibly can so your fellow citizens can be warned in time to combat its next growth spurt. You will also want to formulate a plan for saving the town from the Thing.*

2.  Have students record all the information about the substance on a record sheet. Tell them to be sure to use their five senses and the attribute-listing chart as they describe the unknown object.

3.  Write a newspaper article giving all the pertinent details and a plan for eradicating the menace.

4.  Tell students to try to identify the substance.

## *Notes on Attribute Listing*

Encourage your students to use the attribute-listing chart (page 33) as a guide in the initial phases of their study. Point out the areas that they are missing consistently and show them how to identify and fill in those areas. The chart relieves any concern students might have about remembering the five senses or the major categories, and allows them to feel successful about their initial observations.

When the students have developed keen observation skills and are familiar with the various attributes and categories they can generate, they are ready to make comparisons. For example, they might compare a regular stick of gum with Chewels or bubble gum. Another activity is finding categories that are used over and over for certain kinds of objects or products. For example, what categories are used in describing the nutritional value of foods?

Have the students bring in empty boxes, canned goods, and other food packages to compare terms on the labels.

The following lesson in classifying was originally developed to help teach cursive writing. Our school never seemed to have enough handwriting books, so we used our model to help children see letter similarities and practice cursive at the same time.

# *The Alphabet Conspiracy*

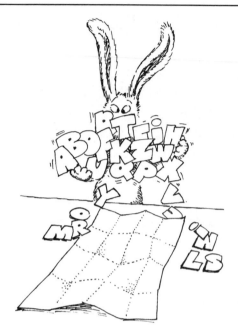

*Tools of the Trade:*
Chalkboard or butcher paper, markers, one piece of paper (8-1/2 by 11) for each student

*Time*
20 minutes

*Problem*
How many ways can you categorize the letters of the alphabet?

*Procedure*

1. Explain the following to the students:

   *Sometimes we suffer from a perception problem called "fixed functionalism." We are so used to looking at something in a certain way that we have difficulty looking at it in a new way. For example, we use letters everyday when we write words. Today I want you to use your creativity to organize those letters in as many different ways as you can.*

2. Have students fold their blank papers in half from top to bottom, then in half again, and finally fold the paper in the middle and in half once more. They should end up with sixteen squares for recording their answers.

3. On the butcher paper or the chalkboard, list the capital letters of the alphabet. Direct students to organize the letters into different groups in the sections of their paper. Some obvious grouping of the letters will occur: curved or straight lines, enclosed spaces, number of "end points," and so on. Other groupings might be vowels, consonants, letters that make blends, letters that join together in a special way in cursive writing, and so on.

# *Phase Four:*
# *Relationship Analysis*

RELATIONSHIP
ANALYSIS

The final phase of the Prolific Thinkers' Teaching Model offers the teacher and students the reward of reaching a finished product through conscious decision making. Relationship Analysis is a synthesis of brainstorming, mind expanders, and connectors. It requires students to project possible outcomes and consequences of decisions they make during the problem-solving process.

An understanding of sequential development and the use of logic are necessary analysis skills that can be taught through flow charts and other visual schematic devices. These devices provide students with visual images that help them think logically and sequentially. Analyzing relationships helps students to

- visualize their solutions;

- rethink problems;

- search for a process that will produce the desired outcome when that outcome is already known (sometimes the only way to reach the solution is to work a problem backward);

- make decisions at the concrete level, where each step can be broken down into simple increments; and

- become familiar with the decision-making process so they are prepared to deal with more abstract and complex problems.

All of us have deferred decisions because there were no guarantees of the results. For example, the stock you are considering as an investment may bring financial loss rather than gain. Risk taking is an inherent part of the decision-making process. Making a good decision requires the ability to project the probable outcome or consequences. To build confidence and skill in decision making, students must develop a clear picture of cause-and-effect relationships and sequential development.

## Mastering the Art of Sequential Development

Rube Goldberg, a cartoonist and a most ingenious inventor of impractical devices, offers some wonderfully improbable schemes using sequential development. Goldberg develops his ideas visually as he unfolds the complicated process that makes his inventions work.

Such unique power sources as a cat chasing a dog, the rays of the sun being focused by a magnifying glass, or rain filling a bucket can trigger a chain of events that surprises and delights the child in all of us. But these flights of imagination have their practical side, for each action is part of a logical chain of cause and effect.

Goldberg's titles tip off the reader to the probable outcome and are prime examples of thinking visually and thinking backward. A new alarm clock for waking up in the morning might consist of a bird catching a fake worm attached to a lever that opens a cage to release a cat that has its tail attached to a rope tied to a pail of water that is suspended over the sleeping person's bed. Students should see a number of these Goldberg-style illustrations so they can appreciate the complex planning (and the fun) that goes into them.

## The Logistics of Visual and Mental Logic

As students work on their own Goldberg-style inventions, they will develop new strategies for problem solving. Because the desired outcome is known at the beginning of the undertaking, the student is forced to examine ways and means of reaching the goal. Remind students that there should always be more than one solution. Lee Iacocca, who became famous as the president of Chrysler Corporation, said that he never accepts one solution to a problem. Before making important decisions, he always wants two or more choices. Students should be sure to consider all alternatives before they settle for one.

## The Role of Fantasy and Imagination

In the world of business, solutions are usually judged by financial profits and losses. Plans and changes in plans are based on market studies that review past trends and project future trends. The ultimate decision whether or not to produce a product could be simply a matter of dollars and cents. In spite of this, fantasy and imagination still play a role in decision making. It's interesting to note that some of the biggest and most successful corporations in America routinely hire "creativity consultants" to help spark and rejuvenate the fantasy and imaginative powers of their employees.

When we work with students on such lessons as "The Goldberg Variations" on page 42, we try to keep in mind that without fantasy and imagination, future inventions may well be overlooked. Science fiction writers have long predicted space travel and life in environments unknown to us today. Your students' current fantasy solutions may be the answers to the serious problems we will face tomorrow.

## *Notes on Inventing a "Rube Goldberg"*

The following suggestions may help students create inventions of their own.

1. Choose a routine task that your invention will do. (Offer the suggestions on page 47 for inspiration.)

2. Think and rethink the sequencing of events necessary to produce the outcome you want.

3. Be creative! Look at your problem from a different angle. Try to gain a new insight into the solution. How can you harness nature to work for you? Consider rain, wind, ocean tides, and so on. Break new ground by discovering new ways of generating power and causing actions and reactions. For example, Goldberg used an electric fan blowing on a block of ice for air-conditioning and gears and levers for motion.

# The Goldberg Variations

RELATIONSHIP
ANALYSIS

*Tools of the Trade*
Scratch paper, drawing paper,
pencils

*Time*
20-minute sessions each day for
a week, or as needed

*Problem*
Invent a new way to catch a
mouse.

*Procedure*

1. Brainstorm a possible sequence of events. If students need help, prompt
   them with such questions as these:

   *What will attract the mouse?*

   *What will actually catch it?*

   *What will the source or sources of power be?*

   *Where will these things be placed?*

2. Encourage students to list elements to be included in their drawing,
   working backward from the final effect.

3. Have students make a rough sketch of these elements and number them in
   order of their use in the invention.

4. Ask students to check the logic of each event by working through the
   sequence of events with a friend.

5. Have students make their final drawings.

*Teacher Tips*

   If your students aren't that familiar with Rube Goldberg cartoons,
create a sample "Goldberg variation" with them, going through all the steps
above. One student-created example appears on the next page.

# HOW TO CATCH A MOUSE

Mouse (A) sees cheese on cylinder and steps on lever (B) to reach cheese, causing string (C) inside cylinder to pull trigger on gun (D), releasing bullet (E), which pops balloon (F), releasing cage (G) overhead, which catches mouse (A) eating cheese.

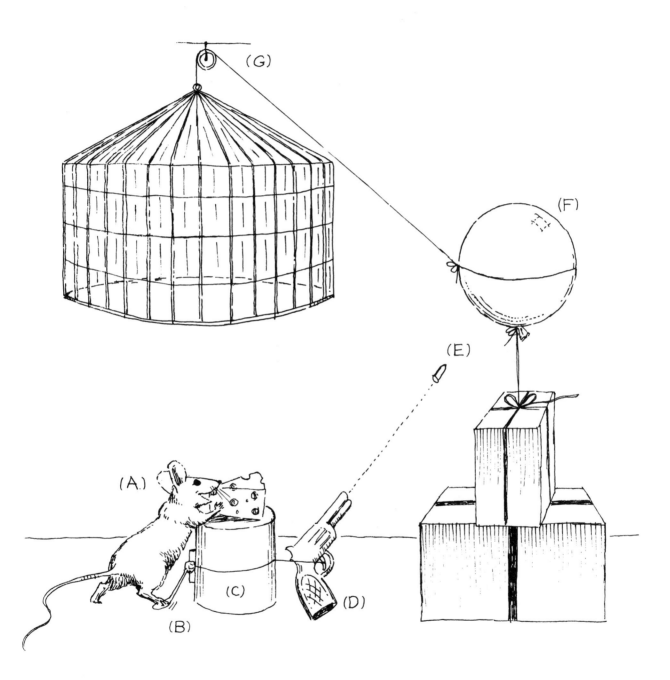

# Flowcharting

Computers and computer technology offer the student a different form of decision making. Writing computer programs requires a planned sequencing of events using a predetermined format. Flowcharting and programming are ways for students to test the logic of their thinking against the results on the computer screen. Adults and children alike can feel themselves stretch mentally to find the missing element in their computer program and make it work.

Whether or not you have a computer, computer symbols have become an acknowledged tool for planning future programs and their implementation. Flowcharting is one aspect of this planning that offers a type of visualization that Rube Goldberg might be using if he were alive today. Who knows, the next lesson might spark the discovery of a high-tech Goldberg in your own class!

## Symbols for a Simple Flowchart

Flowcharting symbols and methods vary greatly. Here are some that you may wish to use. The number of symbols you introduce will depend on the ability range of your students.

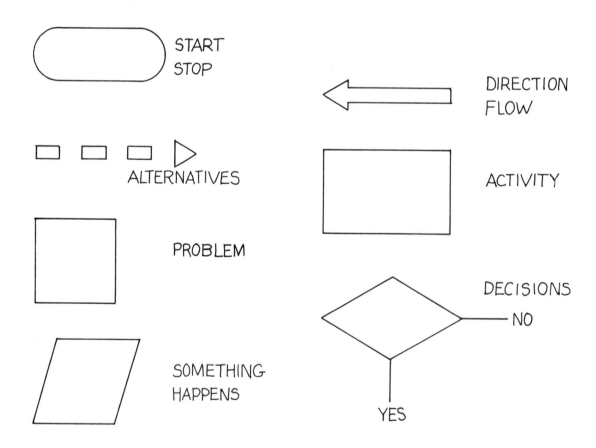

# How to Wash a Rabbit

RELATIONSHIP
ANALYSIS

*Tools of the Trade*
Graph paper, chart illustrating
flowchart symbols

*Time*
20-minute sessions each day for
a week or as needed

*Problem*
Make a flowchart showing the
necessary steps to wash a rabbit.

*Procedure*

1. Review the rules for brainstorming.

2. Have students write out the steps for washing a rabbit. Suggest they use triple spacing so that any steps they miss can be inserted.

3. Have students place the steps in their proper order on a flowchart.

4. Review flowchart symbols; then have students draw appropriate symbols around the steps.

5. Ask students to add directional arrows and alternatives.

6. Have students choose partners and rethink their flowcharts together.

7. When final revisions have been made, students prepare their final product.

*Sample Responses*
One example is illustrated on page 46.

# HOW TO WASH A RABBIT

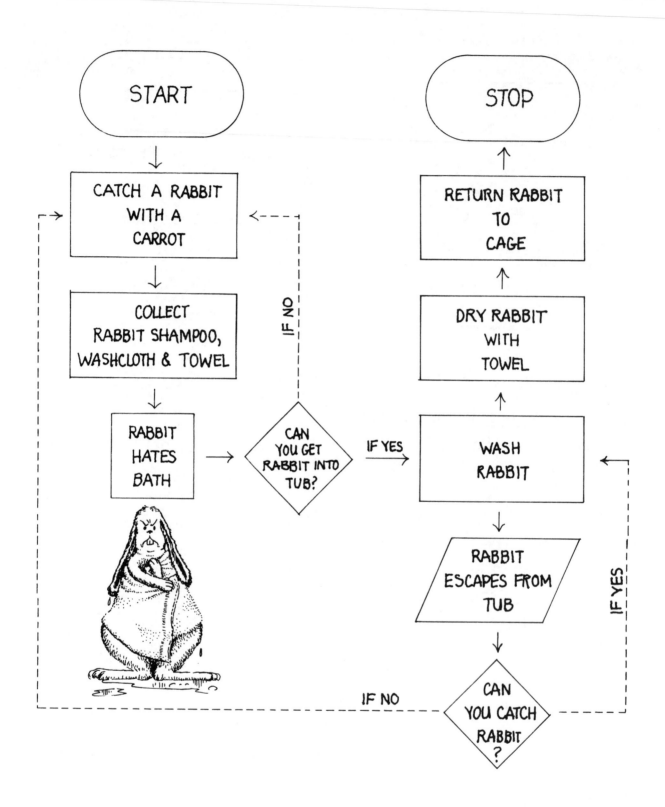

START

CATCH A RABBIT
WITH A
CARROT

COLLECT
RABBIT SHAMPOO,
WASHCLOTH & TOWEL

RABBIT
HATES
BATH

CAN
YOU GET
RABBIT INTO
TUB?

IF NO

IF YES

STOP

RETURN RABBIT
TO
CAGE

DRY RABBIT
WITH
TOWEL

WASH
RABBIT

RABBIT
ESCAPES FROM
TUB

CAN
YOU CATCH
RABBIT
?

IF YES

IF NO

46

# Lessons in Sequential Development

We include here a list of ideas for Rube Goldberg-type drawings and a list of possible subjects for flowcharting. Don't stop with these items; add ideas contributed by your students, your fellow teachers, and your own imagination.

Remember that Rube Goldberg drawings and flowcharting have a lot in common. For a special challenge, have some of your students choose an idea to represent in Goldberg's cartoon fashion *and* as a flowchart. Let them present both ideas to the class and discuss the different kinds of problem-solving techniques they used for each method.

## More Rube Goldberg Ideas

Show an original way to . . .

| | |
|---|---|
| catch a fish. | feed a baby. |
| sharpen a pencil. | scratch your back. |
| feed your dog. | cut your hair. |
| weigh a whale. | vacuum the floor. |
| wash a pet bird. | put a baby to sleep. |
| start a fire. | curl your hair. |
| get yourself up in the morning. | mow the lawn. |

## Additional Ideas for Flowcharts

Make a flowchart to show how to . . .

| | |
|---|---|
| mail a letter. | drive a car. |
| watch a television show. | set a table. |
| check a book out of the library. | shine your shoes. |
| make a peanut butter and jelly sandwich. | run a computer program. |
| wash your clothes. | walk a dog. |

## Matrix Logic

Matrix logic is another form of problem solving that fits into Relationship Analysis because it requires students to break down a problem into many details and then arrange and rearrange those details, according to given clues, to come up with a logical solution. Matrix problems need to be read and reread, and often some determination must be made as to which clues are relevant to the solution of the problem.

There are many commercially available matrix logic problems that your students can use for practice. We like to expose students to these first. Two good collections are *Quizzles* and *More Quizzles* by Wayne Williams (an educational version is available as reproducible blackline masters from Dale Seymour Publications, Palo Alto, Calif.).

To involve some higher-level skills, you can have students write their own matrix problems. This is not as hard as it sounds. After your students have experience in solving matrix problems, have them try writing some very simple ones. As students become more familiar with the requirements of this special problem format, they can develop more complex examples. Writing matrix problems over a period of time, students will develop both in creativity and in their ability to use deductive logic in problem solving.

In the following lesson, "Combing Through the Clues," we offer two sample matrix problems. Problems like these have been making the rounds for a very long time. In fact, these were adapted from some that are over thirty years old! The first problem, "Who Does What?" is somewhat easier to solve than "Who's Who on the Baseball Team?" Both are fairly difficult. For your convenience, answers to "Who Does What?" and "Who's Who on the Baseball Team?" are given below.

---

*Answer Key for "Combing Through the Clues"*

**WHO DOES WHAT?**
Rita is the painter and the counselor.
Sara is the musician and the gas station attendant.
Teresa is the accountant and the gardener.

**WHO'S WHO ON THE BASEBALL TEAM?**
Jesse is the pitcher; Andy is catcher; Bill plays 1st base; Jackson plays 2nd base; Mario plays 3rd base; Otis is shortstop; Jim plays left field; Frank plays center field; and Tomas plays right field.

# *Notes on Solving Matrix Logic Problems*

- Matrix problems are solved by a process of elimination through the accumulation of many pieces of information. It is helpful to use a grid or matrix to keep track of the details as they accumulate. For example, the grid for "Who Does What?" might look like this:

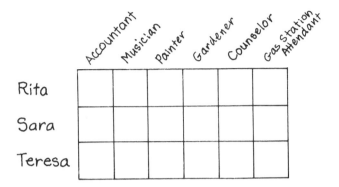

Depending on your students' abilities, you may want to explain the idea of the grid and let them design the specific grid that will work for each problem. After reading the problem through, students can brainstorm the categories they will want represented on their grid.

- For solving a problem with the grid, the standard approach is to place an X in any box that is *not* possible. For example, in "Who Does What?" we learn in clue number 5 that Sara owes the gardener money. Since Sara cannot be the gardener, we put an X in the box on the grid that corresponds to *Sara* and *gardener*.

- After recording in the grid all the facts you pick up from reading through the clues once, start through the clues again and try to discover some answers or eliminate some further possibilities by combining the information. Which clues seem to fit together, or present facts that are related? Search your grid for further clues, too.

- When you discover an answer, write YES or make a big O in the appropriate box on the grid. Each time you enter a YES or an O, you will be able to put an X in certain other boxes on the grid (the ones remaining in that row in either direction). For example, in "Who's Who on the Baseball Team," suppose you were to discover that Mario is the pitcher. [Ed. note: He isn't necessarily.] If Mario is the pitcher, then he cannot play any other position (8 boxes can be X'ed out), and no other player can be the pitcher (8 more boxes can be X'ed out).

# *Combing Through the Clues*

RELATIONSHIP
ANALYSIS

*Tools of the Trade*
Paper, pencil, eraser, copy of the problems

*Time*
Each problem makes a good homework assignment.
Allow as much time as needed over a period of one week.

*Problem*
Solve the logic problems "Who Does What?" (below) and
"Who's Who on the Baseball Team?" (page 51).

*Procedure*

1.  Duplicate the problems and distribute copies to your class.

2.  Encourage students to design grids (charts) that will help them solve each problem.

3.  Remind the students that even with a grid, they will need to read through all the clues two or three times, relating the facts in one clue to the facts in another, before they discover all the information they need to solve the problem.

 – – – – – – – – – – – – – – – – – – – – – – – – – – – – – – – – – –

## WHO DOES WHAT?

There are three women— Rita, Sara, and Teresa— each of whom is engaged in two occupations. Their occupations are: accountant, musician, painter, gardener, counselor, and gas station attendant.

From the following facts, find the two occupations of each woman.

1.  The accountant complimented the musician on her gourmet cooking.

2.  Both the musician and the gardener used to go hiking with Rita.

3.  The painter bought a tankful of gas from the gas station attendant.

4.  The accountant used to date the painter's brother.

5.  Sara owed the gardener $5.00.

6.  Teresa beat both Sara and the painter at a game of Trivial Pursuit.

*Prolific Thinkers' Guide • ©1987 Dale Seymour Publications*

# WHO'S WHO ON THE BASEBALL TEAM?

Listed below are some comments about the nine members of a baseball team. With careful and studious reading and some deductive reasoning, you should be able to figure out which position each man holds on the team.

Each team member plays only one position. In baseball terminology, the battery is the pitcher and catcher. The infield is made up of the first, second, and third basemen and the shortstop. The outfield is made up of the left fielder, the center fielder, and the right fielder.

1. Jesse and the third baseman live in the same building.

2. Otis, Jesse, Frank, and the catcher are usually beaten at golf by the second baseman.

3. Mario is a very close friend of the catcher.

4. The center fielder is taller than the right fielder.

5. The shortstop, the third baseman, and Frank often go fishing together.

6. The pitcher's wife is the third baseman's sister.

7. Bill's sister is engaged to the second baseman.

8. Otis and Andy took the pitcher out to lunch on his birthday.

9. The catcher and the third baseman go camping with their wives and children every summer.

10. Jim is thinking of getting a divorce.

11. All the players in the battery and the infield, except for Andy, Jesse, and Mario, are shorter than Jim.

12. Bill and the outfielders like to play gin rummy together once a week.

13. Jackson is taller than Frank. Tomas is shorter than Frank. Each of them weighs more than the first baseman.

14. One of the outfielders is either Tomas or Mario.

15. Bill, Otis, Jackson, the center fielder, and the right fielder are bachelors. The others are married.

16. Jesse, Mario, and the shortstop don't play gin rummy.

# Prolific Thinking and Problem Solving

People have always been motivated and challenged by the idea of solving problems to improve the world we live in. Real-life problem solving is a complex process. It requires that we examine what we already know, then make intuitive leaps into areas as yet unimagined. Solutions may be inspired by constructing visual models, by observing nature, by searching for analogies and relationships outside the immediate problem's frame of reference. Sometimes the solution just "comes to us" after we let the problem, with all its variables, sit and ferment for a while. There is no single formula for problem solving. Nonetheless, practicing the prolific thinking strategies presented in the four phases of the Prolific Thinkers' Teaching Model can increase the likelihood of finding the best solution.

Studying inventors and their inventions is one way to become acquainted with the creative spirit and to recognize the important part creative thinking plays in arriving at a good solution to a problem. Society today is shaped by the genius and inspired tinkering of the inventor. To illustrate the art of prolific thinking, we offer a final sample unit that integrates the four phases of our teaching model. This unit shows how research and open-ended questioning can result in a stimulating and creative study of problem solving.

## The Inventive Mind

How inventive are you? If you look up the meaning of *invent,* you'll find many of the terms we've been using to discuss critical and creative thinking. At one time the word *invent* meant "to come upon or find." Other definitions use the words *create, devise, imagine, discover,* and *experiment.*

No matter how you define it, the importance of inventing can be verified by history. To prove this point, invite your class to make a time line of some important inventions and imagine what life would be like today if they had never been invented.

# Getting in Touch with Genius

*Tools of the Trade*
Paper, pencils, reference books

*Time*
One class period a day for a week

*Problem*
Make a ranked list of the 25 most important inventions. Decide what categories the inventions fall into and discuss how the world would be different without these inventions.

*Procedure*

1. Students work in small groups. They begin by deciding major categories that inventions tend to fall into. For example, categories might include communication, transportation, medicine, science and industry, agriculture, human conveniences, and so on. Each group lists across the top of a piece of paper the categories they have identified.

2. Each group makes a list of 25 of the most important inventions in our world. The groups then decide what major categories these inventions fall into and write the inventions under the appropriate categories.

3. Each group discusses how the world would be different without these inventions.

4. Each group prepares a presentation for the class that includes a chart showing the inventions in rank order.

5. After all presentations, see how many inventions each group ranked in its top ten. Create a data base to determine the frequency with which the inventions are listed by the various groups.

6. Have students discuss whether adults would list the same inventions. If not, why would adults' lists be different?

*Lesson Extensions*

As a spin-off, have each student choose one invention from the group's list and do research to prepare the following projects:

1. Find out as much as you can about the inventor by reading a biography, letters written by the inventor, and/or newspaper articles about the inventor and his or her work. Can you determine where the inventor got inspiration? Did the inventor keep a notebook of ideas? Or wake up in the night and write down ideas? Or invent as a child? For example, Seymour Papert, the inventor of the computer language Logo, writes that as a child he was fascinated with the way gears moved. In his book, *Mindstorms,* Papert says that these early observations were very important to his future invention.

2. Try to find drawings of the invention before it was manufactured and photographs of the invention now. What changes have been made since the original conception? Present a report to the class showing the original appearance of the invention and its modern appearance. Explain the changes. Then present your own drawings showing improvements you would make based on today's technology.

3. Role play the part of the inventor. Describe your invention and your expectations for it.

4. Create a prospectus for the invention. (A prospectus is a report that is written to interest people in investing money in your idea, so that you can get it manufactured.) Plan an advertising campaign.

5. One well-known inventor, Alexander Graham Bell, invented the telephone while he was trying to make a device to help the deaf. He made the connection between the workings of the human ear and a means to transmit the human voice. His own life provided motivation for his research. Find out what that motivation was.

6. Set up a data base with the information you and your classmates have collected for future research. For example, include the name of the invention, the inventor, the year of the invention, where the invention took place, a description of the invention, a classification for the invention, the impact the invention has had on society, and later inventions that were inspired by this invention. Have each student prepare a record of the invention he or she studied to contribute to a file of information. Use this file to find new information. For example:

    a. Which of the inventors on file is credited with the most inventions?

    b. Was there a year or period of years when more inventions seemed to take place?

    c. Find all inventions that have had an impact on modern-day medical practice.

d. Find all inventors who made major improvements to the airplane.

e. Find all inventions that are part of our space program.

By simply sorting for the right set of data, you can use your class data base to answer numerous complex questions.

## More Inventive Ideas

### A Matter of Time

One of the ultimate challenges to man has always been the control and harnessing of time. Writers and moviemakers have worked with the idea of building a time machine. How would you travel through time?

Draw a set of blueprints for a time machine. You might plan to make it from recycled parts or the ultimate in high technology. Be sure to label all the parts of your machine and tell how it would work.

What era in history would you like to visit? You might want to think of an event in the past and how you could play a part in it. For example, suppose you visited England in 1796. Dr. Edward Jenner is working on the smallpox vaccine but has run into a snag. Tell how you will help him with his discovery.

### Chain of Events

Some inventions change our lives by sparking a chain of related inventions. A good example of this is the laser. Consider how the laser has changed our lives. Today it is used in welding, surgery, typesetting, photoengraving, range finding, art, and videodiscs. The list is still growing. The laser has brought about a number of technological changes. Look at other inventions that have caused a chain of new inventions to appear. What new inventions have been triggered by the invention of the automobile, the microscope, or the telephone?

### The Don't-Be-Alarmed Alarm Clock

Do you hate to get up in the morning? Are you one of those people who snooze "just five minutes more," then another five minutes, and another? Recently we saw an ad in the newspaper for an alarm clock with the latest improvements. This clock had two alarms that could be set for a couple who arise at different times for work. It also had a radio that slowly increased in volume as the minutes passed to ensure a gentle awakening. Despite innovations such as these, the alarm clock really hasn't improved or changed much.

Invent the best possible version of the alarm clock that you can think of. Draw a blueprint and label the parts. Then construct a model of your invention.

### Patent Pending

When a patent is granted, the government guarantees the inventor a monopoly on the invention for 17 years. (According to the patent law, an invention is an idea that has not been thought of before or one that wouldn't be obvious to someone with ordinary skill.)

A patent doesn't guarantee that an idea won't be copied. In fact, the holder of the patent must do the monitoring himself or herself. Some companies never file for a patent, preferring to keep the details secret in hope that their invention will remain exclusively their own. The formula for Coca-Cola is an example of that.

A group of ambitious inventors have started the Inventors Workshop International (IWI) with 30 chapters in the United States and Canada. Take the best invention from your class and contact the IWI about getting it patented. Ask for application blanks and instructions on how to conduct a patent search. If you live in a large city, you can conduct a patent search yourself in the patents room of a major library.

Find out whether any inventors live in your city. If you locate some willing inventors, interview them about their work and their ideas. Prepare your questions carefully beforehand.

### Cliff Hangers

Writers seem like inventors when they place characters in a position from which there seems to be no escape. Here is an exercise in cliff hangers that really stretches your imagination. Take a long piece of shelf paper and write the first part of a story. Make the story as exciting as possible. When you get to an especially exciting point, pass the story on to a friend to write the next part. You can do this five or six times, with each writer trying to stump the next into giving up. Need a starter? Try this:

> *We had been flying over the Everglades for hours searching for the lost plane. Below us I could see the swamp. The grasses seemed harmless, belying the quicksand below. I looked over at*

*José, the pilot, who seemed to have a perpetual scowl on his face,*
*only to see the lines of worry deepen.*
   *"What's the matter, José?" I asked, trying to sound calm.*
   *"There's something wrong with the plane. We're going to*
*have to land somewhere in this swamp."*
   *Before he had finished I felt the plane lurch forward and*
*begin a sickening plunge toward earth. We were going to crash,*
*all right . . . .*


## *Improvements, Modifications, and Minor Adjustments*

Most inventions are minor improvements or changes in devices that already exist. Make a list of items that are simple machines or devices and see what kinds of improvements or modifications you can make. Use SCAMPER to get you going. Here are some sample lists.

To improve the basic electric can opener:

1. Make it battery-powered to free an electrical outlet.
2. Add rubber handles to prevent shock.
3. Include a strainer to remove liquid from the can.
4. Add a lid remover for jars.
5. Add a device to open pop-top drinks.
6. Add a label remover.

To improve eyeglasses:

1. Make the lenses out of a material that won't fog up.
2. Make the frame out of a material that never loses its shape so they always fit perfectly.
3. Make them adjustable, like binoculars, so you can adjust your own vision.
4. Have a radio inside the frame for listening pleasure.
5. Add a TV image that can be projected on the lenses for very nearsighted people.
6. Install stimulators that won't let you go to sleep when you are trying to study.
7. Install stimulators that make the left brain work if you are right-brain oriented.

Now try your inventiveness with some of these: the stove, the bathroom scale, hats, the spoon.

*The Great Inventors' Perpetual Motion Contest*

This is a good activity for people who can express themselves well with models. You have practiced making flowcharts and Rube Goldberg designs, so you are familiar with the process of creating both kinds of models. Are you ready for the ultimate challenge? The perpetual motion machine! Design a machine that uses its own power and momentum to run forever.

1. You may want to experiment with simple machines such as the lever, pulley, inclined plane, wheel and axle, and with balances and counterweights.

2. Decide on a power source. Water, wind, and sun are some ways to get things moving. How about a rubber band and a hand crank?

3. Draw or sketch your plan for a perpetual motion machine. Make a list of the materials you will need to build your machine. Where are the problem areas? Make a flowchart, writing each step of your machine's motion.

4. Now begin building your machine.

5. Have an Inventor's Fair and bring your models. Displays might include your other inventions from "The Classroom Creativity Kit," "The Multipurpose Belt," and drawings and flowcharts from other lessons.

# The Prolific Thinkers' Marathon

The Prolific Thinkers' Marathon provides students with critical and creative thinking problems to be solved by teams in a competitive setting. The problems are structured to require all the participants to play an active role in formulating solutions and implementing the ideas of the team. The goal of the marathon is to provide opportunities for students

- to receive recognition for their ingenious or unique solutions to two problems and their contributions to one extemporaneous brainstorming session;

- to appreciate other students' thinking and to see how others reached their unique and ingenious solutions; and

- to work together in a cooperative fashion in solving complex problems.

## Organization of the Marathon

The marathon is organized around three major problem-solving events: "Strawscrapers," "Mental Gymnastics," and "Time Capsule." These problems represent a synthesis of the critical and creative thinking skills presented to the students throughout the year.

The marathon is organized for team competition. The competition could be among teams in one classroom, or teams could represent classes or schools in a schoolwide or districtwide competition. A team consists of five students. A teacher acts as facilitator to each team, but the team members are responsible for arriving at their own solutions to each problem.

The marathon problems require thought but no expense for their implementation. Materials or props should be readily available within the school or at home.

## The First Event: Strawscrapers

All teams participate at once in "Strawscrapers." It's an exciting event to watch, so be sure to set aside space for spectators. In this activity, students try to build the tallest structure possible out of a given number of drinking straws. The activity gives students an opportunity to build something concrete and to see that there are numerous approaches to solving the problem.

Prior to the actual event, the teams may try out different design ideas and may even practice building their final design many times. This period of experimentation is to be encouraged. During the practice sessions, the teacher or coach should ask questions such as the following to help students think of solutions:

- What is the best way to join two straws?
- How can you make your structure stronger and more stable?
- Does the size of the base of the structure affect the height? How does that affect your planning?
- Can the structure be built in segments?

Since straws vary so much, we usually advise participating teams what brand of straws will be used in the actual marathon so they can be practicing with the same type.

## Setting Up Strawscrapers

*Setup*

Multipurpose room, auditorium, or cafeteria with a defined working space for each team and a spectators gallery. All teams participate in this event at the same time.

*Materials*

For each team:

- Butcher paper approximately 1 meter long
- Sealed envelope with 50 pins
- 50 drinking straws bundled together with a rubber band

*Time Limit*

15 minutes

*Problem*

Using the materials supplied, build a straw structure. The tallest structure that is standing when time is called will win. All structures will be measured and ranked, with standing structures ranked higher than nonstanding structures.

*Procedure*

1. Mark butcher paper with each team's name and place on auditorium floor, leaving plenty of space between teams. Place pins and straws on each piece of paper. All materials remain unopened at this time.

2. Teams meet at their spaces.

3. No coaches are allowed on the auditorium floor at this time. Coaches and spectators are assigned to designated seating areas to view the event.

4. Judges read the rules for the event. (The rules will have been distributed in advance with other information about the marathon.) At a signal from a judge, the materials may be opened and the event begins.

5. When time is called, all building must stop. If a team finishes a structure before time is up, they may stand, but no one may leave the floor until time is called. At that time, all participants must leave the floor, being careful not to disturb any of the structures.

6. After the judges have measured all the structures, all participants return to the floor to dismantle their structures, returning pins to the envelope and replacing straws in the rubber band.

# Judging Strawscrapers

## Judges
Six judges, or two sets of three judges

## Judges' Materials
- Roving (a thick yarn)
- Two pairs of scissors
- Stepladder
- Pencils
- Colored index cards
- Butcher paper 280 centimeters long, marked in centimeters.
- Rules for the event (see appendix, page 80)
- Scoring forms (see appendix, page 81)

## Judges' Procedures

1. One of the judges will read the rules for the event and act as timekeeper.

2. Each judge has a set of colored index cards. During the event judges position themselves so each can see a section of the auditorium floor. When time is called, judges drop the index cards next to all structures that are standing. These structures will be ranked first. Structures that have fallen or could never stand will be ranked after the standing structures. If a structure falls after the judging begins, the judges may make one attempt to restand the structure.

3. Judges measure the structures in the following way: Working in groups of three, one judge holds the roving taut at the base of a structure, while the second judge measures to the top of the structure. The roving is cut and measured against the centimeter tape. The height is recorded. One team measures the standing structures and the other team the nonstanding structures. Judges turn over the results to a scorekeeper for ranking based on the height.

   Winners are announced after the final tally is complete. All participants are ranked, but you may choose to announce only the top three teams at this time.

## The Second Event:  Mental Gymnastics

"Mental Gymnastics" is a team brainstorming session. Teamwork is vital because all of the team members depend on each other to keep the flow of ideas going. Each team member must give a response when his or her turn comes. No one is allowed to pass. If one member is stuck, the whole team is stuck.

This is one event where practice throughout the year really pays off. Students who have practiced the application of SCAMPER and the ABC Connection will find a response, no matter what the brainstorming problem presents.

# Setting Up Mental Gymnastics

## Setup
A separate room with a table and five chairs arranged in a semicircle. Only one team will participate at a time. Two chairs are set opposite the team for the judges. A chair for the coach is provided, behind the team. A timekeeper and an optional recorder sit off to one side.

## Materials
- Brainstorming item or word
- A stopwatch
- A tape recorder (optional)

## Time Limit
1 minute to think about topic, 3 minutes to brainstorm

## Ahead-of-Time Note
When scheduling this event, assign two teams to each 15-minute time block. This will allow the judges time to average each team's score after their brainstorming session.

## Problem
Brainstorm ideas about the topic that is presented to you without stopping or repeating ideas. Each team member must respond in turn. Points are given for the number and creativity of responses. Team with the highest point total will win.

## Procedure

1. The timekeeper meets the team at the door. Upon entering the room, the team is invited to sit at the table in the order in which they plan to respond. The captain of the team is identified and the team tells the two judges who will respond first. The timekeeper can also operate the recorder if the judges wish to record each team's responses. The rules for "Mental Gymnastics" are read. (These will have been distributed in advance as part of the problem packets given to teams six weeks prior to the marathon.)

2. Only team members and one coach will be allowed in the competition area; no spectators are allowed for this event.

# Judging Mental Gymnastics

## Judges
Two judges and one timekeeper

## Judges' Materials
- Pencils
- Rules for the event (see appendix, page 82)
- Scoring forms (see appendix, page 83 and 84)

## Judges' Procedures

1. On each judge's scoring form, list team names in order of appearance or in alphabetical order.

2. Read the rules for the event to the participants.

3. Judges read the problem to be solved or hand the object to brainstorm to the first respondent.

4. A timekeeper starts the stopwatch to measure the one-minute thinking session. At the end of the minute, the timekeeper says "Go," and the three-minute response time begins.

5. Judges record tally marks on the scoring form as responses are given. If any answer is given more than once, judges say "Repeat," and the participant must give another response.

6. At the end of the three-minute session, the timekeeper says "Stop," and the event is over.

7. The team leaves the room while the judges transfer their results to the Mental Gymnastics Final Tally form and record the team's final score. A final ranking is established when all teams have completed the event.

## Optional

You may wish to tape record each team's responses in case of a question as to whether a response was in fact duplicated. The tape backup provides you with instant verification. The trade-off is time, which becomes a problem in a large marathon with many participants. Judging is not an exact science. The human factors are simply part of the competition.

## The Third Event: Time Capsule

"Time Capsule" is the only problem that may involve some research. In this problem the students collect materials representative of their own culture for inclusion in a time capsule. For purposes of the marathon, "their own culture" can be defined as covering the time period from five years ago to the present in the location where they are currently living. Equally as important as the final selection of objects is the written documentation and rationale that must be provided to the judges prior to the marathon.

# Setting Up Time Capsule

## Setup

Stage or designated area for the presentations. Groups will present their time capsules one at a time.

## Materials

- Teams will provide their own materials for the presentation.
- Large name cards for each team
- Chart stand for the team name cards

## Time Limit

This is a two-part activity.

- Documentation: Due before marathon begins; exact date to be set by judges.
- Presentation: 2 minutes to set up, 3 minutes to deliver

## Ahead-of-Time Note

Judges for this event must meet prior to the marathon to judge the documentation written by the students about each time capsule.

## Problem

Make a time capsule that will let people of the future know what our society is like today. Choose objects from the last five years that you feel reflect our way of life. When you have agreed on what will go into the capsule, prepare documentation to accompany it. This will be a listing of each item in the capsule, along with a rationale for its inclusion. The problem should not be overdefined by coaches or facilitators. The problem of how to complete the documentation should be interpreted and solved by the students.

## Procedure

1. Each team has two minutes to set up the presentation. A timekeeper will indicate when the presentation must begin.

2. The team has three minutes to present the time capsule to the three judges and the audience.

# Judging Time Capsule

*Judges*

Three judges

*Judges' Materials*

- Pencils
- Stopwatch
- Scoring forms (see appendix, pages 86-88)

*Judges' Procedures—Documentation*

1. The documentation is judged in advance. We suggest that the judges first read through all the documentation provided by the teams. Then the judges should divide the documentation into four categories: outstanding, good, average, and below average. During a second reading, point scores can be assigned. The highest possible score is 100 points. Use the judge's documentation scoring form (page 86) to record each team's results. The final scores are also recorded on the presentation scoring form (page 87).

2. The documentation is judged on creativity, format, and variety. Creativity is worth a possible 50 points and format and variety 25 points each. Thus the total possible score for documentation is 100 points. Creativity refers to the overall originality and creative thinking that went into solving the problem. This is a very subjective category. After reading through all of the documentation, the judges will begin to see varying degrees of creativity. Format refers to the completeness, organization, and clarity of the documentation. Variety refers to the range of items selected. The wider the range of appropriate items, the higher the score.

*Judges' Procedures—Presentation*

1. Judges will rate each team's presentation on creativity, format, and variety. Possible point scores are the same as for documentation: 50 for creativity, and 25 each for format and variety. These scores are added to the documentation score. A maximum of 200 total points can be earned in this event. Each judge's individual scores for this event are transferred to the Time Capsule Final Tally form. A final ranking is established when all teams have completed the event.

2. Penalties can be given to teams that do not follow the rules. If penalties are used, judges should decide on them and inform participants before the marathon. For example, 10 points might be deducted for going over the time allotment for setting up.

68

## Final Scoring for the Marathon

To minimize confusion, assign one or two judges to prepare the final tally sheet that determines the winners of the marathon. In addition to the Prolific Thinkers' Marathon Final Tally Sheet, the judges will need only three forms that have been filled out for the individual events: the Strawscrapers Scoring Form, the Mental Gymnastics Final Tally, and the Time Capsule Final Tally. After listing the teams in alphabetical order, judges should transfer each team's numerical ranking in the individual events to the final tally form and add these rankings to find each team's total. Now a final ranking can be determined, from lowest to highest total points. That is, the *winning* team is the one with the *lowest* number of total points.

## Coaching

Within a classroom, the teacher can act as coach. In a larger marathon, you may want to enlist the help of parent volunteers as coaches. We advise having a separate meeting with the coaches to present the marathon problems and to answer questions. It is also advisable to caution parents about the role of a coach in any competition.

The solutions the students find may not be the ones that a coach or teacher would find. The role of the coach is to provide not *answers* but *questions*. For example, if a straw structure is not standing, it would be appropriate to ask, "How can we change the base to offer better support?" It would *not* be appropriate to say, "Let's change the shape of the base to a square," or "Let me show you how I'd do it."

Given enough time, each team will arrive at a satisfactory solution. The frustration level will be high if students do not have adequate planning or preparation time. Remember, it takes time to learn how to think and work as a team.

The team will need the coach's encouragement and appreciation of their efforts along the way, especially during slow periods. Learning how to sustain momentum is an aspect of problem solving that can make or break a team. The students may reach plateaus and become frustrated by their lack of progress. By asking provocative questions at such a time, the coach can be helpful without interfering.

The marathon problems were designed to be solved over a period of time. Allow at least six weeks between the formation of the teams and the actual marathon. Encourage the teams to meet weekly to work on their problems and practice their presentations. You may wish to draw up a time line for the activities that will lead up to the marathon.

*Time Frame for the Prolific Thinkers' Marathon*

1. Pick a date for the Prolific Thinkers' Marathon. Arrange for a room or rooms and janitorial staff for that day. (This may have to be done months in advance.) We have used a multipurpose room for our marathons. Order any trophies, ribbons, and certificates you may need.

2. Schedule time at a faculty meeting to describe the marathon and announce its date.

3. Set a date for a teacher and parent-volunteer in-service training session. Prepare copies of the problems, information about the marathon, and registration information, to be handed out at the in-service sessions. (See sample forms in the appendix.)

4. At the in-service training session, present the marathon events in detail. Practice brainstorming and building strawscrapers if time permits. Bring samples of straws, straight pins, and time capsule box to show participants.

5. Write a letter to parents describing the marathon. Be sure to include date and times. Prepare permission slips for participation if necessary. Send home letters about the event with the parent permission slips.

6. Form teams. Present marathon problems to the teams. Hold a class discussion of the events at this time to be sure all the participants understand the rules. If you are having a schoolwide or districtwide competition, hold an informational meeting for all participants.

7. Hold the first practice session. Students may want to build strawscrapers during this practice session.

8. Encourage student teams to establish a regular schedule of planning and practice sessions over the next six weeks. Provide meeting time for these sessions during class.

9. Send out registration forms to participants. (See sample registration form in the appendix.)

10. Contact judges for each event. It is best that judges not be connected with the schools or classrooms that are participating. Plan a judges' training session before the marathon. This session can be combined with the judging of the "Time Capsule" documentation.

11. Write a general bulletin about the marathon for distribution on the day of the event. This bulletin should describe each event and the rules under which the event is being conducted.

12. When the registration forms have been received, schedule the teams for each event. The first event is "Strawscrapers." All teams participate at the same time in a large space. The second and third events, "Mental Gymnastics" and "Time Capsule," are held at the same time. List teams in random order, drawing names out of a hat. Schedule two teams for each 15-minute time period. Stagger the times so that a team will do "Mental Gymnastics," have a break of 15 minutes, and then perform "Time Capsule."

13. Assign judges to individual events. Sample score sheets appear in the appendix. All judges can judge the "Time Capsule" documentation in advance. This offers them a chance to work together in an informal setting and answer any questions they might have prior to the marathon. We usually make this session an informal dinner meeting; everyone has a great time and the group comes together as a team of judges.

14. The day before the marathon, set up all materials, equipment, and supplies. Arrange judges' tables, scoring materials, and supplies in the proper locations. We always make a large welcoming banner and supply refreshments for the kids and the parents. Post signs for restrooms, parking, and so on, as needed.

15. Conduct the marathon.

Although each problem is exciting taken on its own, the marathon as a whole is a special experience. The students, parents, and coaches have been unfailingly enthusiastic about the marathon, whether or not their teams have won the events. The results of teamwork are frequently inspiring, and the sportsmanship is outstanding. Again we emphasize that we are not meeting just to judge a competition, but to appreciate the results of a lot of hard work and a lot of critical and creative thinking.

After running marathons for students at both school and district levels and even a marathon for adults, we have come up with some suggestions for a trouble-free event.

1.  **If this is your first marathon, limit the number of teams to 20.** This will be plenty to handle. Increase the number of teams only if you are sure that room and energy permit. Limiting the size may mean holding a marathon just for upper grades, or just for eleventh graders. Decide all of these limits in advance.

2.  **Make a list of all the things you will need for the marathon.** Use your list as a check-off sheet. You will need trophies, ribbons, certificates, team packets, schedules, judging folders, a microphone or public-address system, several stopwatches, clipboards, tables for registration and refreshments, chairs, trash cans, a stepladder, lengths of butcher paper, straws counted out in groups of 50, pins counted out in groups of 50 and sealed in envelopes, scissors, string or roving, a centimeter tape, a brainstorming object, and a hand-held calculator. You will probably need some extension cords, a banner, and some signs. We even ask a calligrapher to be present to correct any errors in certificates on the spot!

3.  **Identify one person who will answer all questions.** To prevent confusion, just one person should be the marathon "referee" who answers any questions about rules and procedures. Let all participants know who that person is and how he or she can be reached. Make it clear that this individual is the *only* person who interprets rules or procedures. This person should be alert to the fact that many participants ask questions in an effort to find out "what the judges are looking for" in the response to a marathon event. In most cases we simply refer the participant back to the rules. To give *any* hints or clues would suggest that there is only one right answer, which defeats the purpose of the marathon.

4.  **Plan what you will do in case of a tie.** Announce in advance your tie-breaking strategy. The way we suggest scoring the marathon, ties unfortunately do occur. For example, if a team scored a first place in "Strawscrapers," a second place in "Mental Gymnastics," and a fifth place in "Time Capsule" their total would be 8 (1 + 2 + 5). Another team that scored a third place in "Strawscrapers," a fourth place in "Mental Gymnastics," and a first place in "Time Capsule" would also score 8 (3 + 1 + 4). We break such ties by referring back to the "Strawscraper" event, selecting the team with the higher standing structure as the winner.

5. **Set up the night before the marathon.** This takes about three hours. We hang a large banner that says "Welcome to the Prolific Thinkers' Marathon." Arrange tables to be used for registration and refreshments. Fill coffee pots with water and check electrical outlets. Hang signs for bathrooms, parking, and so on.

6. **Prepare for setting up chairs.** We set up chairs around the room in a U shape. We print the team names and schools on pieces of butcher paper and place them around the area the teams will use to build the straw structures. After the strawscrapers have been judged and taken down, we move the chairs into rows to get ready for the "Time Capsule" presentation.

7. **Have a moderator who is knowledgeable about the marathon.** The pace of the marathon is fast and furious. Have one person moderate from a microphone. Have another answer all questions from teams and parents.

8. **Arrange for refreshments.** During the first and second events, while the judges are measuring the structures, we take a short refreshment break. This gives the judges time to work and gives the teams a chance to take care of any last-minute preparation for the other events. We always have cookies and milk for the participants, with extras for brothers and sisters who have come to watch. It's a small expense and adds a nice touch. We also supply coffee for adults. We put six refreshment tickets in each packet at registration (for the team members and the alternate). You might make a parent committee responsible for the refreshments.

9. **Make folders for each event, one for each judge.** We place a marathon schedule on the cover of each folder, as well as in each team packet. The folder for the "Mental Gymnastics" event, for example, would contain a schedule, a copy of the event's rules, and a copy of the judging form. We make these forms in advance, share them with the judges before the event, and pass them out on the day of the marathon.

10. **Make sure that all participants are winners.** Before announcing the winning teams, call up each team and have each coach introduce the team members, including alternates. Present a certificate to each team member and alternate, as well as the coach.

# Some Final Thoughts
# on Prolific Thinking

As we come to the end of the *Prolific Thinkers' Guide,* we would like to leave you with the following ideas.

- We believe that students will increase their critical and creative abilities and their productivity through brainstorming and the other steps outlined in our Prolific Thinkers' Teaching Model.

- Students need opportunities to practice making their own decisions. Role playing and simulations are some of the ways we recommend for practicing decision making.

- Socialization is a skill that all students need to put their ideas into practice. Cooperative learning techniques are a necessary part of teaching in all curriculum areas. The Prolific Thinkers' Marathon gives students an opportunity to solve problems in group situations and develop new skills in human relations.

- Critical and creative thinking is an ongoing process that frees our minds to imagine the impossible and perform the unimagined. The Prolific Thinkers' Marathon is an opportunity for young people to compete mentally, trying to become the best they can be. We need mental stars as well as athletic stars. The marathon is one way of offering alternatives and choices for young people.

- Prolific Thinking is a philosophy of teaching. By teaching students how to analyze problems, recognize patterns, and seek alternative solutions, we show them that a major part of learning is learning how to learn. We try to impart to our students the idea that *facts* are not so important in isolation; it is *how you use them* in a learning situation that counts.

To all our many friends, colleagues, and associates who have attended our workshops, in-service training sessions, and marathons, and who have read this manual, we extend our thanks. We are all contributing to better teaching, and therefore to a better society. Thanks for becoming Prolific Thinkers!

## THE PROLIFIC THINKER'S AWARD

The final reward for prolific thinking will go to you, the classroom teacher who doesn't allow a good idea to go to waste. Your classroom is the one that children can't wait to get to every morning. When the students see you in the schoolyard, they come over to share their latest idea or brainstorm.

Or you may be the parent who stretches your children's imaginations while driving to school, brainstorming unusual ways to spend your weekend.

We as a society will benefit from your work when we have creative and ingenious leaders who never say "I can't," but rather, "Let me think!"

# Appendix:
## Prolific Thinkers' Marathon Forms

This appendix includes forms similar to those that we have used for our Prolific Thinkers' Marathon. If you like, you may duplicate these and fill in the appropriate dates, times, and other information. Alternatively, you may simply use these forms as models and modify them to suit your own situation.

Prolific Thinkers' Marathon Announcement          78

Marathon  Registration Form          79

Strawscrapers:  Event Number 1 Rule Sheet          80

Strawscrapers Scoring Form          81

Mental Gymnastics:  Event Number 2 Rule Sheet          82

Mental Gymnastics Scoring Form          83

Mental Gymnastics Final Tally          84

Time Capsule:  Event Number 3 Rule Sheet          85

Time Capsule Documentation Scoring Form          86

Time Capsule Presentation Scoring Form          87

Time Capsule Final Tally          88

Prolific Thinkers' Marathon Final Tally Sheet          89

# PROLIFIC THINKERS' MARATHON

## ANNOUNCEMENT

**TIME:** Registration at _____

First event begins promptly at _____

Award Ceremony at _____

**PLACE:** _____

**DIRECTIONS:** _____

**DRESS:** Casual clothing

**FOR MORE INFORMATION CONTACT:** _____


## GENERAL TEAM RULES

1. Teams will consist of five students.
2. There will be two divisions of competition.
   Primary Division:  Team members may be in grades 1, 2, and 3.
   Upper Division:  Team members may be in grades 4, 5, and 6.
   If any member of the team is in an upper division grade, the entire team will be considered in the upper division category.
3. Teams must compete in all events.

## GENERAL COMPETITION RULES

1. All decisions of the judges are final.
2. All teams must register by _____.
   Please use the attached registration form.
   Mail to_____
3. Note that Event Number 3, "Time Capsule," requires that you send documentation along with the registration form. Be sure to include this.
4. Each team must have its team name and school name on display during the competition.
5. All time restrictions will be strictly observed or penalties will be incurred by the team.
6. *Only* team members will be allowed in competition areas. Coaches and spectators must remain in the specified viewing areas during the competition.

Prolific Thinkers' Guide • ©1987 Dale Seymour Publications

# PROLIFIC THINKERS' MARATHON
# REGISTRATION FORM

Please mail by _____ to _____

Don't forget to include the documentation as required in Event Number 3.

Name of school_____

School address_____

Telephone number_____

Contact person at your school_____

Name of coach_____

Please list the team members.  Certificates will be prepared from this list.
Please check the spelling and print all names.

Team name_____

1. _____Grade_____

2. _____Grade_____

3. _____Grade_____

4. _____Grade_____

5. _____Grade_____

Alternate team member  _____ Grade_____

This problem is given in advance.
Teams are encouraged to practice.

# STRAWSCRAPERS

**PROBLEM:** What is the highest structure you can build with 50 straws and 50 pins?

**MATERIALS:** 50 plastic drinking straws, 50 straight pins

**TIME LIMIT:** 15 minutes

## RULES

1. Only the materials supplied may be used.

2. Structures must be freestanding.

3. No chairs or stepladders will be permitted for safety reasons.

4. Structures that fall after time is called may be subject to the following guidelines:
   a. Judges may ask the team to attempt to stand the structure.
   b. Judges may attempt to stand the structure.

5. All structures will be measured. Standing structures will be ranked first, in order of height. Nonstanding structures will be ranked below standing structures, also in order of height.

6. Judges will be allowed to lay the structure flat on the floor for measurement and scoring if necessary.

# Strawscrapers
# Scoring Form

| Team Name | Height (cm.) | Standing? | Rank* |
|-----------|--------------|-----------|-------|
|  |  |  |  |
|  |  |  |  |
|  |  |  |  |
|  |  |  |  |
|  |  |  |  |
|  |  |  |  |
|  |  |  |  |
|  |  |  |  |
|  |  |  |  |
|  |  |  |  |
|  |  |  |  |
|  |  |  |  |
|  |  |  |  |
|  |  |  |  |
|  |  |  |  |
|  |  |  |  |
|  |  |  |  |

*Rankings to be transferred to Prolific Thinkers' Marathon Final Tally Sheet.

Only the rules for this event are given out in advance. The actual problem will not be known until the time of competition.

---

# MENTAL GYMNASTICS

**PROBLEM:**  Presented by the judges at the time of the event.

**MATERIALS:**  To be provided by judges as needed.

**TIME LIMIT:**  1 minute to think, 3 minutes to respond.

## RULES

1. The judges will present the problem to the team. Team members should immediately begin thinking of as many responses as they can. After one minute of "thinking time," the event will begin. The team will have three minutes to give responses.

2. Each team member must respond in turn. No team member may skip a turn or repeat a previous answer. If a response is given more than once, judges will call out "Repeat" and the participant will have another chance to respond. The team continues to respond until time is called or until a team member is stalled. If one team member is stuck, the whole team is stuck.

3. The team will receive 5 points for each common (ordinary) response. Creative responses will receive 10 points.

4. Only team members and one coach will be allowed in the Mental Gymnastics competition area. No spectators will be allowed.

## SAMPLE PROBLEMS (FOR PRACTICE)

1. Examine an unknown object provided by the judges and state its function.
2. Name as many things as you can that are both sharp and wooden.
3. Name as many things as you can that will float in a tub of water.
4. Name as many kinds of tables as you can. Some common responses might include a dining room table, a night stand, or a wooden table. Some creative responses might include a table of contents, times tables, or a tabled motion.

# Mental Gymnastics
# Scoring Form

| Team Name | Common (5 points) | Creative (10 points) | Total* |
|---|---|---|---|
|  |  |  |  |
|  |  |  |  |
|  |  |  |  |
|  |  |  |  |
|  |  |  |  |
|  |  |  |  |
|  |  |  |  |
|  |  |  |  |
|  |  |  |  |
|  |  |  |  |
|  |  |  |  |

*These scores to be transferred to Mental Gymnastics Final Tally form.

# Mental Gymnastics
# Final Tally

| Team Name | Judge 1 | Judge 2 | Total | Rank* |
|-----------|---------|---------|-------|-------|
|           |         |         |       |       |
|           |         |         |       |       |
|           |         |         |       |       |
|           |         |         |       |       |
|           |         |         |       |       |
|           |         |         |       |       |
|           |         |         |       |       |
|           |         |         |       |       |
|           |         |         |       |       |
|           |         |         |       |       |
|           |         |         |       |       |

*Rankings to be transferred to Prolific Thinkers' Marathon Final Tally Sheet.

Teams must prepare their presentations in advance.

# TIME CAPSULE

**PROBLEM:** Prepare a time capsule. Select the artifacts that will give the truest reflection of this country's culture and lifestyle of the last five years. Prepare documentation describing each item you include and explain why you selected it.

**MATERIALS:** To be gathered by students prior to the event.

**TIME LIMIT:** Documentation is due _____.

**PRESENTATION:** 2 minutes to prepare, 3 minutes to deliver

**RULES**

1. Each team prepares a time capsule. All artifacts must fit into a cardboard box, about the size of a "banker's box" or a box that ditto paper comes in.

2. Teams prepare a documentation list to be submitted along with the registration form. The list must name all the items in the capsule and a statement explaining why each item was included.

3. Team presentations may be communicated in song, dance, poetry, drama, and so on.

4. Background settings and flats must be collapsible and easy to transport. All must be handled, designed, and set up by team members.

5. All costumes and props should be designed and fully executed by the team members.

6. A placard must be visible stating the name of your school and team name during the performance.

7. Judging will be based on the documentation (100 possible points, scored in advance) and performance at the marathon, which is broken down into creativity—includes costumes, artifacts, and scenery (50 points), format (25 points), and variety (25 points). Please note: A substantial penalty will be applied to teams who fail to file their documentation as stated above.

8. Keep in mind that the performance event will take place in a cafeteria setting where there is no stage, microphone, or electrical connections.

9. The intention of Prolific Thinkers' Marathon is that no cost should be incurred by team members. Ingenuity and school or found materials should suffice.

# Time Capsule
# Documentation Scoring Form

Scored Prior to the Marathon

| Team Name | Creativity (50 points possible) | Format (25 points possible) | Variety (25 points possible) | Total* (100 points possible) |
|---|---|---|---|---|
| | | | | |
| | | | | |
| | | | | |
| | | | | |
| | | | | |
| | | | | |
| | | | | |
| | | | | |
| | | | | |
| | | | | |
| | | | | |
| | | | | |

*These scores to be transferred to Time Capsule Presentation Scoring Form.

Prolific Thinkers' Guide • ©1987 Dale Seymour Publications

# Time Capsule
# Presentation Scoring Form

| Team Name | Documentation (scored prior to the event) (100 points possible) | Performance | | | Total* (200 points possible) |
| --- | --- | --- | --- | --- | --- |
| | | Creativity (50 points possible) | Format (25 points possible) | Variety (25 points possible) | |
| | | | | | |
| | | | | | |
| | | | | | |
| | | | | | |
| | | | | | |
| | | | | | |
| | | | | | |
| | | | | | |
| | | | | | |
| | | | | | |
| | | | | | |
| | | | | | |
| | | | | | |

*These scores to be transferred to Time Capsule Final Tally.

# Time Capsule
# Final Tally

| Team Name | Judge 1 | Judge 2 | Total | Rank* |
|-----------|---------|---------|-------|-------|
|           |         |         |       |       |
|           |         |         |       |       |
|           |         |         |       |       |
|           |         |         |       |       |
|           |         |         |       |       |
|           |         |         |       |       |
|           |         |         |       |       |
|           |         |         |       |       |
|           |         |         |       |       |
|           |         |         |       |       |
|           |         |         |       |       |

*Rankings to be transferred to Prolific Thinkers' Marathon Final Tally Sheet.

Prolific Thinkers' Guide • ©1987 Dale Seymour Publications

# Prolific Thinkers' Marathon
## Final Tally Sheet

| Team Name | Rank Order in Individual Events | | | Total | Rank |
|---|---|---|---|---|---|
| | Strawscrapers | Mental Gymnastics | Time Capsule | | |
| | | | | | |
| | | | | | |
| | | | | | |
| | | | | | |
| | | | | | |
| | | | | | |
| | | | | | |
| | | | | | |
| | | | | | |
| | | | | | |
| | | | | | |
| | | | | | |
| | | | | | |

# Selected References

Eberle, B. *SCAMPER: Games for Imagination Development.* Buffalo, N.Y.: DOK Publishers, Inc., 1971.

Edwards, B. *Drawing on the Right Side of the Brain.* Los Angeles: J. P. Tarcher, Inc., 1979.

Feldhusen, J. F., and D. J. Treffinger. *Creative Thinking and Problem Solving in Gifted Education.* Dubuque, Iowa: Kendall/Hunt Publishing Company, 1981.

Gowan, J. C., J. Khatena, and E. P. Torrance. *Creativity: Its Educational Implications.* Dubuque, Iowa: Kendall/Hunt Publishing Company, 1981.

Guilford, J. P. *Intelligence, Creativity, and Their Educational Implications.* San Diego, Calif.: Robert R. Knapp, 1968.

———. *The Nature of Human Intelligence.* New York: McGraw-Hill Book Company, 1967.

Myers, R. E., and E. P. Torrance. *Invitations to Thinking and Doing.* Boston: Ginn and Company, 1964.

Noller, R. B. *Scratching the Surface of Creative Problem Solving: A Bird's Eye View of CPS.* Buffalo, N.Y.: DOK Publishers, Inc., 1979.

Osborn, A. F. *Applied Imagination.* New York: Charles Scribner's Sons, 1963.

Parnes, S. J. *Creative Behavior Guide Book.* New York: Charles Scribner's Sons, 1967.

Ricca, J., and D. J. Treffinger. *Adventures in Creative Thinking.* Buffalo, N.Y.: DOK Publishers, Inc., 1982.

Stanish, B. *Hippogriff Feathers.* Carthage, Ill.: Good Apple, Inc., 1981.

Torrance, E. P. *Creativity.* Belmont, Calif.: Fearon Publishers, 1969.

———. *Guiding Creative Talent.* Englewood Cliffs, N.J.: Prentice-Hall, 1963.

Torrance, E. P., and R. Myers. *Creative Learning and Teaching.* New York: Dodd, Mead, 1970.